BOSTON
Like a Local

BOSTON
Like a Local

BY THE PEOPLE WHO CALL IT HOME

Contents

NIGHTLIFE

OUTDOORS

meet the locals

MEAGHAN AGNEW

Boston-born Meaghan lives and breathes the city's sports teams and foodie scene. When she's not writing about the latest brunch offering, she can be found smelling the flowers in the Boston Public Garden.

CATHRYN HAIGHT

Writer and editor Cathryn has called Boston home for six years. You'll find her buying antiques, ordering extra tzatziki at Greek restaurants, and wandering Back Bay, book in hand.

JARED RANAHAN

Freelance writer Jared was raised in Middleboro, Massachusetts. His work takes him across the world, but he feels most at home in the Bay State. In his free time, he enjoys long bird-watching sessions and drinking craft beer.

Boston

WELCOME TO THE CITY

Established way back when, in 1625, Boston is one of the oldest cities in the US. During its long history, this coastal port has provided a safe harbor for folks seeking a new life, including freedom seekers on the Underground Railroad, Irish and Italian immigrants, and later arrivals from the likes of Jamaica and Colombia. Open-armed and open-minded, that's Boston. This city has long been a hotbed of radical, boundary-pushing ideas. As any Bostonian will tell you, this was the birthplace of the American Revolution and a key player in Abolitionism. And it's progressive movements like these that have given Boston a reputation for being free-thinking and forward-looking.

Little has changed since the city's early days: Boston is still a creative, barrier-breaking place, thanks in no small part to its large student population (we see you Harvard, MIT, and MassART) and switched-on, community-minded locals. Across Boston, you'll find countless spots challenging norms, whether it's inclusive bookstores packed with diverse reads, offbeat theaters hosting thought-provoking performances, or trendy wine bars serving up responsibly sourced wines. The city's inhabitants are fierce in their support of these locally run businesses, just as they are with teams like the Red Sox, Bruins, and Celtics (Boston has an undying love for sports, don't you know?).

When it comes to it, Bostonians are – and have always been – what make this place what it is. Who better, then, than these passionate folks to show you their beloved city? Whether you're a local looking for something new or a first-time visitor hoping to see the real side of Boston, we're sure you'll find something special in these pages. So, pull on a Sox jersey and get in among the best of them. This is Boston, by its people.

Liked by the locals

"I love that you can always discover places that feel like home in Boston. For me, that's the packed shelves at Beacon Hill Books & Cafe, the dock on the Charles River Esplanade on a chilly day, and a window table at Kava – with a side of zucchini chips, of course."

CATHRYN HAIGHT, WRITER AND EDITOR

Spring blossoms, summer foodie festivals, and a crowd-rousing sporting event for every season – there's always something afoot in Boston.

Boston
THROUGH THE YEAR

SPRING

A CITY IN BLOOM
Locals know spring has well and truly sprung when the magnolia trees in Back Bay and South End shed their petals like snow, dusting the city in pale pink.

BOSTON MARATHON
One of the world's "Big 6" marathons, this iconic event draws runners from all over. Locals cheer from the sidelines or watch the action from bars.

LILAC SUNDAY
You'll see locals taking their ma for a stroll and a picnic among the stunning lilacs in the grounds of the Arnold Arboretum *(p165)* on Mother's Day (the only day in the year when this is allowed).

ST. PATRICK'S DAY
Ireland's patron saint is celebrated all over town, culminating in a lively parade. Locals go all out, so grab a Guinness and go wild with the best of 'em.

SUMMER

SOX SEASON
Any sport-loving Bostonian worth their salt is obsessed with the Red Sox. Come summer, Fenway Park *(p178)* is packed to the brim with hot dog-munching fans.

PICNICS BY THE CHARLES
The Charles River Esplanade is popular year round, but never more so than in summer, when friends and families come to dine alfresco in this waterside park.

BEACH BASH

With temperatures rising, locals flee the city for sandy shores. Handily, there are lots of beaches just a short T ride away, where folks can laze in the sunshine, drinks in hand, or cool off with a dip in the sea.

ST. ANTHONY'S FEAST

On the last weekend of August, foodies flock to the city's Italian North End to gorge themselves on hot arancini, sweet cannoli, and mammoth pizza slices – all in the name of St. Anthony.

FALL

HEAD OF THE CHARLES

This three-day regatta – the largest in the world – has been a Boston tradition since the 1960s. Spectators line the bridges and banks of the Charles River to watch the world's best rowers in action.

STUDENTS RETURN

Every fall, Boston comes alive with an influx of enthusiastic students ready to start the new semester. There's a certain buzz in the air, especially in Cambridge, where folks from Harvard and MIT crowd into cafés and bars.

FOOTBALL SEASON

Football is a religion in Boston, and the New England Patriots are its patron saints. Sundays see fans glued to screens in bars, ready to celebrate or commiserate depending on the result.

LEAF PEEPING

With fall comes an explosion of color. Boston Common *(p165)* and the quaint streets of Beacon Hill are favorite spots for leaf-peeping locals to catch the show.

WINTER

HOLIDAY MARKETS

After Thanksgiving, holiday markets crop up around the city. A favorite is the one in SoWa, which shoppers browse while sipping hot cocoa.

ICE SKATING

As the snow begins to fall, skaters of all ages come to glide across the fairy light-encircled Frog Pond in Boston Common.

BRUINS AND B-BALL

During winter, die-hard hockey and basketball fans descend on TD Garden *(p177)* for Bruins and Celtics games – beers in hand, of course.

There's an art to being a Bostonian, from the do's and don'ts on a night out to negotiating the city's winding streets. Here's a breakdown of the essentials.

Boston

KNOW-HOW

For a directory of health and safety resources, safe spaces, and accessibility information, turn to page 186. For everything else, read on.

EAT
Boston is packed with great places to eat out, from cozy Italian trattorias to long-standing seafood spots. Lunch is often on the go, but brunch and dinner are bigger affairs, where locals catch up with friends or family. There's little need to make a reservation during the week, but they're a must come the weekend, especially for trendy joints in the South End and Back Bay. Oh, and no need to dress up: most places are pretty casual.

DRINK
Coffee shops are big hubs in Boston: locals will linger here for hours, either with a laptop or a friend. As for alcohol,

the city is famous for its breweries, which craft big-name beers and local suds alike, and for its sports bars packed with loyal fans. Making a mark more recently on the city's drinking scene are natural wine bars and cocktail joints. Plan to arrive early (5–6pm) at these places, since many are walk-in and fill up fast; same goes for sports bars on game days. One last thing: it's illegal to take your drinks out onto the street.

SHOP
Whether they're buying gifts, garments, or groceries, Bostonians love keeping it local when it comes to shopping. The South End and Beacon Hill neighborhoods both have a big concentration of indie businesses. Stores are usually open from 9 or 10am to 6 or 7pm daily; some extend their hours on Friday and Saturday. It's worth carrying a tote, as

you'll be charged 5 cents for a recyclable, compostable, or reusable bag (single-use plastic bags are banned).

ARTS AND CULTURE

Museums can get pricey in Boston, with many charging upward of $20. The good news? You can get a no-cost dose of history by strolling one of the city's many themed walking routes, such as the Black Heritage Trail *(p116)*. Most art galleries don't charge, and the SoWa arts district hosts free openings of its studios and galleries every first Friday of the month (wine and cheese included).

NIGHTLIFE

Nightlife in Boston is pretty relaxed. Locals tend to kick back in pubs and bars (clubs are few and far between), or catch a comedy show, indie theater performance, or live music sesh. Unsurprisingly, this means folks dress casual. Don't expect a late night: places close by 2am here (it's the law). A heads-up: keep your ID handy, as well as some cash (some places have a cover charge).

OUTDOORS

Come summer, Bostonians flock to the city's parks and beaches to stroll, cycle, and picnic. There are lots of trash cans and recycling bins dotted about, so do your part to help keep these outdoor spaces clean (plus, you can be fined $20 if you're caught littering). Squirrels and seagulls can be brazen when it comes to grabbing a snack, so keep yours out of reach.

Keep in mind

Here are some more tips and tidbits that will help you fit in like a local.

» **Tip well** Adding at least 20 percent to your bill is a must at bars and restaurants.

» **Carry cash** Most of the city is contactless, but some bars accept only cash, so keep some handy.

» **Keep hydrated** Coffee shops often have self-serve water dispensers where you can top off.

» **No smoking** Smoking is banned inside public buildings and in parks. While the purchase and use of cannabis is allowed, it's illegal to smoke it in public.

GETTING AROUND

One of the oldest cities in the US, Boston was built from a patchwork of smaller settlements. A tightly packed collection of historic areas can be found to the north of the city, with more expansive neighborhoods extending out to the south. Many of the older areas have winding and somewhat convoluted streets, but thankfully navigating them isn't too difficult as these neighborhoods are so small.

Despite being cities in their own right, some surrounding areas like Cambridge and Somerville are considered part of the larger Metro Boston Region by virtue of their proximity to Boston.

To help you get around, we've provided what3words addresses for each sight in this book, meaning you can quickly pinpoint exactly where you're heading.

On foot

Boston is one of the most walkable cities around. In central Boston, nothing's more than 30 minutes away by foot. The rest of the city is equally walkable, if you have the time and endurance (it'd take a few hours to cross the whole town). Sidewalks in historic districts like the South End and Beacon Hill can be narrow and bumpy, so be mindful of uneven bricks

and cobblestones. Always wait for the walk signal at traffic lights; drivers can sometimes be impatient and may turn even if walkers technically have right-of-way. The locals tend to walk fast, so if you need to check your phone or a what3words location, step to the side.

On wheels

Bostonians love to cycle, whether to work, a coffee date, or just for the fun of it. A recent initiative has led to more bike lanes popping up across the city, making getting around on two wheels easier and safer than ever. After more info? The City of Boston has a handy page on cycling safety and a link to current route maps.

Bluebikes, the city's bike-sharing program, has over 4,000 bikes and 400 docking stations across the city. Buy a pass at the kiosk or download one via the app. A 30-minute trip costs $2.95, with every additional 30 minutes costing an extra $4. There's also the Adventure Pass, which costs $10 and gives you 24 hours of Bluebike access (though bikes must be redocked every two hours), as well as monthly and annual membership plans.
www.boston.gov/departments/
boston-bikes/boston-bike
www.bluebikes.com

By public transportation

The MBTA is Boston's public transit system. It's made up of a subway (known to locals as "the T"), commuter rail, and bus system that services the central city and beyond, as well as several ferry routes. While the system is efficient, the subway can incur delays. If you're standing (a strong likelihood during rush hour), hold onto a handrail as these trains are known for coming to screeching halts.

To pay fares across the whole MBTA network, use a reloadable CharlieTicket, available from one of the subway station vending machines. A single bus trip costs $1.70, the subway $2.40, and the train and ferry from $2.40 upward, depending on the distance you're going. Around for a week? Load your ticket with a 7-day pass for $22.50.

By car and taxi

In the city center, a lack of parking and lots of traffic make getting around by car difficult, so it's only worth driving if you really have no alternative. Cabs aren't common here, so if you do need a car, Uber or Lyft are the most popular choices. For longer jaunts, especially outside of the city, you can rent a car from the airport.

Download these

We recommend you download these apps to help you get about the city.

WHAT3WORDS

Your geocoding friend

A what3words address is a simple way to communicate any precise location on earth, using just three words. ///fills.bars.festivity, for example, is the code for Boston's John F. Kennedy Presidential Library and Museum. Simply download the free what3words app, type a what3words address into the search bar, and you'll know exactly where to go.

MBTA MTICKET

Handy transportation app

If you're using Boston's commuter rail or the ferry, then download the MBTA mTicket app. Not only can you check schedules and read service alerts, you can also purchase tickets easily.

Boston is a patchwork of distinct neighborhoods, each with its own unique personality. Here we take a look at some of our favorites.

Boston
NEIGHBORHOODS

Allston/Brighton

Often lumped together, these neighboring districts are the stomping ground of young professionals and students. Expect dive bars, thrift shops, and an eclectic food scene. *{maps 4/6}*

Back Bay

One of Boston's prettiest neighborhoods, Back Bay is famed for its neatly gridded streets (a rarity in Boston) and gorgeous Victorian brownstones. Swing by for the Bay's swanky bars. *{map 5}*

Beacon Hill

With its old-school gaslit streetlamps and row houses, this spot feels frozen in time. The turf of well-to-do families

and professionals, it's also a magnet for tourists, who come for the charming boutiques and streets. *{map 1}*

Brookline

Located minutes from Back Bay, this patch is technically its own little city. Expect a mix of young professionals seeking a slower pace and lifelong Brookliners who live in stately houses on tree-lined streets. *{map 3}*

Cambridge

We know: Cambridge is its own city and not strictly part of Boston. But located just a bridge away, locals will happily hop between the two. Home to some of the most prestigious universities in the US, including Harvard

and MIT, it's a big hangout spot for students. *{map 4}*

Chinatown

Set up in the early 1800s, this area is home to a diverse and tight-knit community. It also has some of the best restaurants in the city, many of them family run. *{map 2}*

Dorchester

Boston's biggest neighborhood is also its most diverse. Here, grizzled Irish American pubs sit alongside decades-old Vietnamese diners and bustling Bangladeshi restaurants. *{map 5}*

Downtown

Long a hub of business and government, this busy district is packed with historic sights. Tourists drop by to trek down the city's iconic Freedom Trail. {map 1}

East Boston

Separated from the rest of the city by Boston Harbor, Eastie is undergoing rapid development. Despite this, the area has a strong community vibe. In-the-know locals can't get enough of the Latin American food scene. {map 6}

Fenway

As the home of Fenway Park, this neighborhood has long been synonymous with baseball. The vibes are electric on Red Sox game days, but there's plenty more to keep you busy, including two of the city's most iconic art museums. {map 3}

Jamaica Plain

Called JP by locals, this dynamic area has become a hub for creatives who flock to its chic bars and indie shops. Its popularity has led to gentrification, however, which has rapidly priced out many of the area's residents. {map 5}

North End

First settled in the 1630s, the North End is one of the city's oldest spots. Known as Boston's Little Italy, its narrow maze of streets is lined with more pizzerias and cannoli shops than you can shake a stick at. {map 1}

Roslindale

Residential Roslindale flies under the radar, even for many Bostonians. But its loyal residents love it for its community vibes, mom-and-pop joints, and cool brewery. {map 6}

Roxbury

This historically Black neighborhood plays host to a slew of amazing Black-owned businesses. It's also a center for arts and music – don't miss the live jazz and soul performances. {map 5}

The Seaport

Just 20 years ago, this area comprised little more than parking lots and shipping containers. But a flurry of development has seen it morph into one of the city's best nightlife spots. {map 5}

Somerville

Brimming with natural wine bars, feminist bookstores, and comedy clubs, this trendy area is a haven for forward-thinkers. {map 4}

South Boston

Home to immigrants in the early 1900s, Southie has a strong Irish heritage. A recent influx of 20-somethings has turned the area into a bar-hopping hub – a quality that some locals feel is sucking the communal life out of the neighborhood. {map 5}

South End

Once Boston's unofficial "gayborhood," this area is now a hub of ultra-hip restaurants and boutiques. It's also a playground for artsy locals thanks to SoWa, a series of old warehouses converted into studios and galleries. {map 2}

West End

Sport is the name of the game here. Come the winter season, jersey-clad fans flock to the West End's TD Garden to cheer on the Celtics and Bruins. {map 1}

Boston

ON THE MAP

Whether you're looking for your new favorite spot or want to check out what each part of Boston has to offer, our maps – along with handy map references throughout the book – have you covered.

LEXINGTON

MA-2

WALTHAM

WATERTO

US-20

WAYLAND

US-20 WESTON

I-95

WEST NEWTON

I-90

SAXONVILLE

COCHITUATE

I-90

I-90

WELLESLEY HILLS

NEWTON

MA-9

MA-9

MA-9

WELLESLEY

O H

NATICK

FRAMINGHAM

NEEDHAM

I-95

0 kilometers   4

0 miles   4

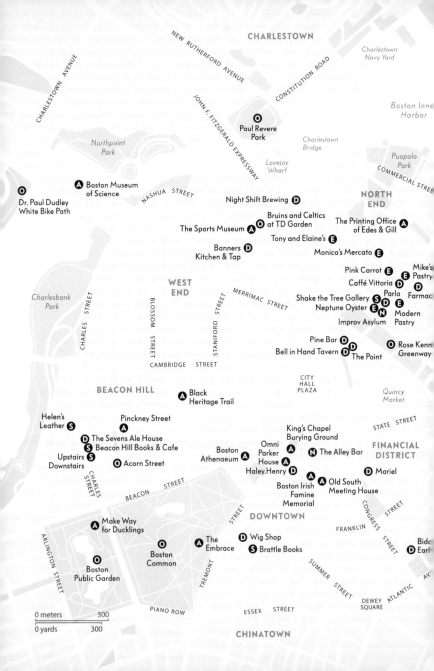

MAP 1

1

E EAT

James Hook & Co. *(p37)*
Mike's Pastry *(p49)*
Modern Pastry *(p49)*
Monica's Mercato *(p43)*
Neptune Oyster *(p38)*
Pink Carrot *(p43)*
Tony and Elaine's *(p46)*

D DRINK

Banners Kitchen & Tap *(p76)*
Bell in Hand Tavern *(p60)*
Biddy Early's *(p60)*
Caffé Vittoria *(p81)*
Farmacia *(p70)*
Haley.Henry *(p65)*
Mariel *(p71)*
Night Shift Brewing *(p72)*
Parla *(p70)*
Pine Bar *(p71)*
The Point *(p79)*
The Sevens Ale House *(p61)*
Wig Shop *(p68)*

S SHOP

Beacon Hill Books & Cafe *(p89)*
Brattle Books *(p89)*
Helen's Leather *(p107)*
Shake the Tree Gallery *(p102)*
Upstairs Downstairs *(p96)*

A ARTS & CULTURE

Black Heritage Trail *(p116)*
Boston Athenaeum *(p131)*
Boston Irish Famine Memorial *(p116)*
Boston Museum of Science *(p124)*
The Embrace *(p132)*
King's Chapel Burying Ground *(p118)*
Make Way for Ducklings *(p134)*
Old South Meeting House *(p117)*
Omni Parker House *(p130)*
Pinckney Street *(p128)*
The Printing Office of Edes & Gill *(p129)*
The Sports Museum *(p127)*

N NIGHTLIFE

The Alley Bar *(p149)*
Improv Asylum *(p147)*

O OUTDOORS

Acorn Street *(p173)*
Boston Common *(p165)*
Boston Harborwalk *(p172)*
Boston Public Garden *(p164)*
Bruins and Celtics at TD Garden *(p177)*
Dr. Paul Dudley White Bike Path *(p168)*
Paul Revere Park *(p167)*
Rose Kennedy Greenway *(p167)*

Battery Wharf

Union Wharf

Lewis Wharf

Boston Harborwalk

WATERFRONT

Rowes Wharf

James Hook & Co.

Evelyn Moakley Bridge

MAP 2

2

SUMMER STREET

acenote

E O Ya

ffsuit

DORCHESTER AVENUE

E EAT

Anoush'ella *(p41)*
B & G Oysters *(p39)*
Blackbird Donuts *(p51)*
Chilacates *(p41)*
Flour *(p48)*
FoMu *(p48)*
Frenchie *(p33)*
Kava Neo-Taverna *(p38)*
Mike and Patty's *(p35)*
Mike's City Diner *(p33)*
Mistral *(p53)*
O Ya *(p52)*
Saltie Girl *(p39)*
Stillwater *(p35)*
Tatte *(p51)*

D DRINK

The Delux *(p61)*
Gracenote *(p82)*
Greystone *(p80)*
Jaho Coffee *(p83)*
Offsuit *(p69)*
Shojo *(p68)*

S SHOP

Artefact Home *(p101)*
Formaggio Kitchen *(p109)*
Hudson *(p100)*
Lekker Home *(p101)*
Marie Galvin Millinery *(p105)*
M. Flynn *(p104)*

Michelle Mercaldo *(p106)*
More Than Words *(p91)*
Ore by Sophie Hughes *(p105)*
Stitch and Tickle *(p104)*
SoWa Vintage Market *(p97)*
Urban Grape *(p108)*

A ARTS & CULTURE

Boston Public Library Central Branch *(p130)*
Don't Let Me Be Misunderstood *(p133)*
Edgar Allan Poe Statue *(p128)*
Gibson House Museum *(p127)*

N NIGHTLIFE

The Beehive *(p155)*
Cathedral Station *(p151)*
Club Café *(p148)*
Jacques' Cabaret *(p150)*
The Kartal *(p150)*
Lyric Stage Company *(p157)*
Nick's Comedy Stop *(p145)*
Speakeasy Stage Company *(p156)*
Trophy Room *(p148)*
Urbanity Dance *(p158)*

O OUTDOORS

Berkeley Community Garden *(p164)*

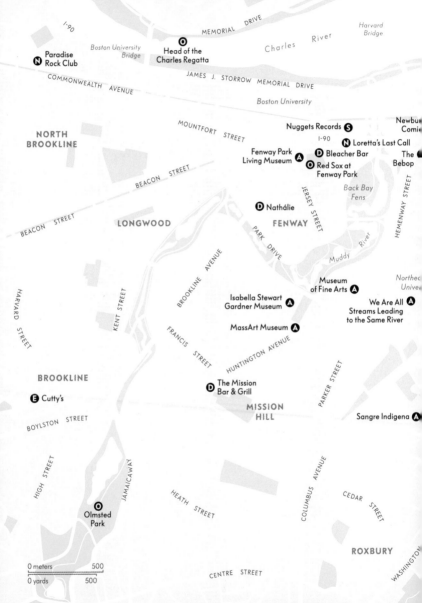

MAP 3

Charles River
Esplanade ◉

3

ommonwealth ◉
Avenue Mall

Rick Walker's
S **E** Select Oyster
N
Cafe 939   BACK
            BAY

Mapparium

HUNTINGTON AVE

Front Porch
N Arts Collective

lly's Cafe **N**
Jazz Club
yl's Corner **N**
& Kitchen   Mida **E**

ONT STREET

ELNEA CASS BOULEVARD

Ramsay
Park

S Frugal
Bookstore

WARREN STREET

E EAT
Cutty's *(p40)*
Mida *(p55)*
Select Oyster *(p38)*

D DRINK
Bleacher Bar *(p79)*
The Mission Bar & Grill *(p78)*
Nathálie *(p67)*

S SHOP
Frugal Bookstore *(p88)*
Newbury Comics *(p93)*
Nuggets Records *(p92)*
Rick Walker's *(p97)*

A ARTS & CULTURE
Fenway Park Living Museum *(p119)*
Isabella Stewart Gardner Museum *(p121)*
The Mapparium *(p125)*
MassArt Museum *(p120)*
Museum of Fine Arts *(p120)*
Sangre Indigena *(p135)*
We Are All Streams Leading to the Same River *(p135)*

N NIGHTLIFE
The Bebop *(p155)*
Cafe 939 *(p141)*
Darryl's Corner Bar & Kitchen *(p155)*
Front Porch Arts Collective *(p158)*
Loretta's Last Call *(p153)*
Paradise Rock Club *(p142)*
Wally's Cafe Jazz Club *(p140)*

O OUTDOORS
Charles River Esplanade *(p171)*
Commonwealth Avenue Mall *(p174)*
Head of the Charles Regatta *(p178)*
Olmsted Park *(p172)*
Red Sox at Fenway Park *(p178)*

DAVIS SQUARE **E** Shirley
S Niche
The Rockwell **N**
N The Comedy Studio

S
Curio
Spice Co.

CEDAR STREET
MEDFORD STREET
BROADWAY

HIGHLAND AVENUE

ELM STREET

MASSACHUSETTS AVE

NORTH
CAMBRIDGE

WINTER
HILL

TOAD **N** PORTER SQUARE

SUMMER STREET

SPRING HILL

Bagelsaurus **E**

HAMPSHIRE STREET

MASSACHUSETTS AVENUE

D Dear Annie

SOMERVILLE STREET

SOMERVILLE

S Pod

N Lizard Lounge

Aeronaut Brewing Company **D** **D**

Wine Bar at Tasting Counter

Filomena
Demarco
Jewelry

S **E** Celeste
Rebel Rebel **D** **S** Crane and Turtle
Wild Child **S**
S **E** Field & Vine
Blue
Bandana Relics

KIRKLAND STREET

American Repertory Theater
N

Cambridge Common
Harvard University

CAMBRIDGE STREET

PROSPECT ST

Alden & Harlow **E** **N** Club Passim
Planet **S**
Records
D Charlie's Kitchen

Armageddon Shop

Parlor Sports **D**
1369 Coffeehouse **D** **N** Lilypad
Zuzu's Petals **D**

Anderson Bridge

Charles

MASSACHUSETTS AVENUE

BROADWAY

CAMBRIDGE

SOLDIERS FIELD ROAD

River

PROSPECT ST

HAMPSHIRE ST

E Oleana

O Crimson at Harvard Stadium

Lord Hobo
D Cambridge

Pammy's **E**

Cambridge City Hall **A**

Cicada
Coffee Bar **D**

D Lamplighter Brewing Co.

E Life Alive

Mamaleh's
E

WESTERN AVENUE

The Garment District **S**

BROADW

Western Avenue Bridge

ImprovBoston **N** **N** Mad Monkfish
Phoenix Landing **D** **E** Veggie Galaxy
N

Vest

RIVER STREET

MAIN STREET

ALLSTON

Central Square Theater

Scullers Jazz Club **N**

River Street Bridge

MASSACHUSETTS AVENUE

M.I.T.

0 meters   600
0 yards   600

CAMBRIDGEPORT

BROOKLINE STREET

VASSAR STREET

Briggs Field

Alchemist **A**

Harvard Bridge

MAP 4

4

E EAT

Alden & Harlow *(p54)*
Bagelsaurus *(p32)*
Celeste *(p52)*
Field & Vine *(p55)*
Life Alive *(p40)*
Mamaleh's *(p42)*
Oleana *(p53)*
Pammy's *(p54)*
Shirley *(p42)*
Veggie Galaxy *(p44)*

D DRINK

1369 Coffeehouse *(p81)*
Aeronaut Brewing Company *(p75)*
Cicada Coffee Bar *(p80)*
Charlie's Kitchen *(p63)*
Dear Annie *(p64)*
Lamplighter Brewing Co. *(p72)*
Lord Hobo Cambridge *(p73)*
Parlor Sports *(p77)*
Phoenix Landing *(p78)*
Rebel Rebel *(p65)*
Vester *(p82)*
Wine Bar at Tasting Counter *(p67)*
Zuzu's Petals *(p64)*

S SHOP

Armageddon Shop *(p92)*
Blue Bandana Relics *(p98)*
Cambridge Antique Market *(p99)*
Crane and Turtle *(p102)*

Curio Spice Co. *(p111)*
Filomena Demarco Jewelry *(p107)*
The Garment District *(p98)*
Niche *(p100)*
Planet Records *(p95)*
Pod *(p102)*
Wild Child *(p88)*

A ARTS & CULTURE

Alchemist *(p133)*
Cambridge City Hall *(p118)*
MIT Museum *(p127)*

N NIGHTLIFE

American Repertory Theater *(p158)*
Central Square Theater *(p156)*
The Comedy Studio *(p147)*
Club Passim *(p140)*
ImprovBoston *(p144)*
Lilypad *(p143)*
Lizard Lounge *(p142)*
Mad Monkfish *(p152)*
The Rockwell *(p145)*
Scullers Jazz Club *(p143)*
TOAD *(p153)*

O OUTDOORS

Crimson at Harvard Stadium *(p176)*
Kayak on the Charles River *(p170)*

BROADWAY

EAST
SOMERVILLE

ASHINGTON STREET

Cambridge
Antique Market S

BRIDGE STREET

EAST
CAMBRIDGE

BINNEY STREET

Kayak on the
Charles River O

MIT Museum O

MORIAL DRIVE

Charles River

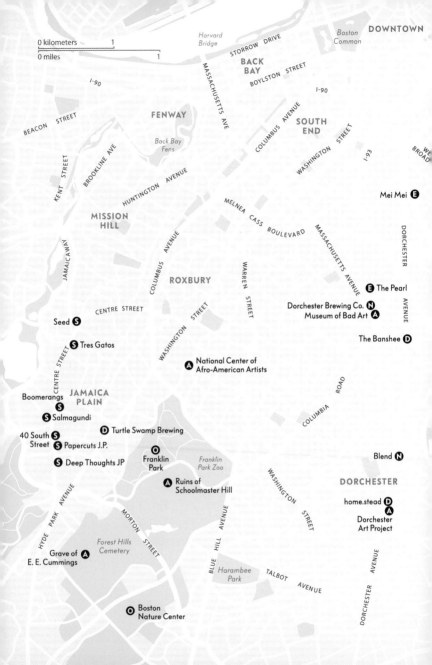

DOWNTOWN

Harvard Bridge

STORROW DRIVE

Boston Common

BACK BAY

BOYLSTON STREET

I-90

I-90

BEACON STREET

FENWAY

Back Bay Fens

MASSACHUSETTS AVE

COLUMBUS AVENUE

SOUTH END

WASHINGTON STREET

I-93

WE BROAD

KENT STREET

BROOKLINE AVE

HUNTINGTON AVENUE

MELNEA CASS BOULEVARD

Mei Mei **E**

MISSION HILL

JAMAICAWAY

COLUMBUS AVENUE

ROXBURY

WARREN STREET

MASSACHUSETTS AVENUE

DORCHESTER

CENTRE STREET

WASHINGTON STREET

E The Pearl

Dorchester Brewing Co. **N**
Museum of Bad Art **A**

The Banshee **D**

Seed **S**

S Tres Gatos

A National Center of Afro-American Artists

ROAD

COLUMBIA

AVENUE

CENTRE STREET

Boomerangs

JAMAICA PLAIN

S Salmagundi

40 South Street **S**

S Papercuts J.P.

D Turtle Swamp Brewing

S Deep Thoughts JP

O Franklin Park

Franklin Park Zoo

Blend **N**

DORCHESTER

WASHINGTON STREET

A Ruins of Schoolmaster Hill

home.stead **D**
A
Dorchester Art Project

HYDE PARK AVENUE

MORTON STREET

Forest Hills Cemetery

Grave of **A**
E. E. Cummings

BLUE HILL AVENUE

Harambee Park

TALBOT AVENUE

WASHINGTON STREET

DORCHESTER AVENUE

O Boston Nature Center

MAP 5

Committee
E
A
Institute of
Contemporary Art

EAPORT

5

N
Laugh
Boston

Stats Bar
and Grill
D
L Street
coln   Tavern
vern   **D**
SOUTH
BOSTON

Carson
Beach

John F. Kennedy
Presidential
Library and Museum
A
*University of
Massachusetts
Boston*

W. T. MORRISSEY BOU

O Tenean
Beach

I-93

O
Joseph
Finnegan Park

E EAT

Committee *(p35)*
Lincoln Tavern *(p32)*
Mei Mei *(p45)*
The Pearl *(p36)*

D DRINK

The Banshee *(p77)*
home.stead *(p83)*
L Street Tavern *(p63)*
Stats Bar and Grill *(p76)*
Turtle Swamp Brewing *(p73)*

S SHOP

40 South Street *(p99)*
Boomerangs *(p96)*
Deep Thoughts JP *(p95)*
Papercuts J.P. *(p91)*
Salmagundi *(p106)*
Seed *(p108)*
Tres Gatos *(p93)*

A ARTS & CULTURE

Dorchester Art Project *(p123)*
Grave of E. E. Cummings *(p129)*
John F. Kennedy Presidential Library
and Museum *(p125)*
Institute of Contemporary Art *(p121)*
Museum of Bad Art *(p123)*

National Center of Afro-American
Artists *(p123)*
Ruins of Schoolmaster Hill *(p131)*

N NIGHTLIFE

Blend *(p151)*
Dorchester Brewing Co. *(p149)*
Laugh Boston *(p145)*

O OUTDOORS

Boston Nature Center *(p175)*
Carson Beach *(p171)*
Franklin Park *(p167)*
Joseph Finnegan Park *(p168)*
Tenean Beach *(p170)*

0 kilometers 3
0 miles 3

MELROSE

WINCHESTER

⊙ Middlesex
Fells Reservation

US-1

I-93

BROADWAY

US-3

MEDFORD

PLEASANT STREET

MALDEN

ARLINGTON

MA-16

EVERETT

REVERE

MA-2

PLEASANT STREET

US-1

MA-1A

Stereo Jack's
Records ⑤

Sylvester Baxter
⊙ Riverfront Park
⑤ All She Wrote Books

PLEASANT STREET

EHChocolatier ⑤

SOMERVILLE

GrayMist Studio ⑤
and Shop

EAST
BOSTON

Death to
Plastic Ⓐ Ⓔ El Peñol

Ⓔ Santarpio's

Arax Market ⑤

WATERTOWN

Boston
Comedy Club

CAMBRIDGE

Ⓓ Downeast
Cider

The Koji Club Ⓓ Ⓝ

BOSTON

Boston Pride at
⊙ Warrior Ice Arena

I-90

Roadrunner Ⓝ

Ⓝ O'Brien's Pub

BRIGHTON

Ⓐ

See maps 1–5
for Central Boston

Sullivan's Ⓔ

Rita's Ⓝ
Spotlight

Brighton
Music Hall

I-90

SOUTH
END

Ivory Pearl Ⓔ

⊙
Pleasure
Bay

SOUTH
BOSTON

BROOKLINE

BEACON STREET

I-93

BOYLSTON STREET

OAK
HILL

JAMAICA
PLAIN

DORCHESTER

Arnold Arboretum ⊙

VETERANS OF FOREIGN WARS PARKWAY

ROSLINDALE

Distraction Ⓓ
Brewing Co.

WEST
ROXBURY

Patriots at Gillette Stadium
↙ ⊙ 14 miles (22 km)

MATTAPAN

I-93

MAP 6

6

MA-1A

 Revere Beach

WINTHROP

Deer Island Nipmuc Memorial  **A**

Boston Harbor

○
Boston Harbor Islands National and State Park

○ **Spectacle Island**

Quincy Bay

E EAT

El Peñol *(p46)*

Ivory Pearl *(p37)*

Santarpio's *(p44)*

Sullivan's *(p46)*

D DRINK

Distraction Brewing Co. *(p75)*

Downeast Cider *(p75)*

The Koji Club *(p67)*

S SHOP

All She Wrote Books *(p91)*

Arax Market *(p111)*

EHChocolatier *(p111)*

GrayMist Studio and Shop *(p103)*

Stereo Jack's Records *(p95)*

A ARTS & CULTURE

Death to Plastic *(p134)*

Deer Island Nipmuc Memorial *(p119)*

Rita's Spotlight *(p132)*

N NIGHTLIFE

Boston Comedy Club *(p147)*

Brighton Music Hall *(p142)*

O'Brien's Pub *(p152)*

Roadrunner *(p141)*

O OUTDOORS

Arnold Arboretum *(p165)*

Boston Harbor Islands National and State Park *(p170)*

Boston Pride at Warrior Ice Arena *(p178)*

Middlesex Fells Reservation *(p173)*

Patriots at Gillette Stadium *(p177)*

Pleasure Bay *(p175)*

Revere Beach *(p169)*

Spectacle Island *(p174)*

Sylvester Baxter Riverfront Park *(p169)*

EAT

*Boston's foodie scene goes way
beyond lobster rolls and clam
chowder. Here, you'll find veggie
fast-food joints, beloved bakeries,
and old-school Italian trattorias.*

Breakfast and Brunch

*Whether it's students capping off a moonlight study
sesh or friends debriefing after a night out, locals love
their morning eats. And with breakfast sandos, fluffy
pancakes, and more on offer, who can blame them?*

BAGELSAURUS

**Map 4; 1796 Massachusetts Avenue, Cambridge;
///speaks.frosted.moon; www.bagelsaurus.com**

There's always a line at the brilliantly named Bagelsaurus. The horde
of hungry hopefuls are here for slow-fermented bagels, made with a
decades-old sourdough starter. All the offerings are deliciously chewy,
but the sea salt bagel with honey-roasted cream cheese is our fave.

LINCOLN TAVERN

**Map 5; 425 W Broadway, South Boston; ///tinsel.sample.pulse;
www.lincolnsouthboston.com**

Come Sunday, Lincoln is packed with bleary-eyed 20-somethings
(who were probably sipping craft cocktails at the bar here the night
before). Girls with messy topknots and bros in backward baseball

Make a resy in advance at Lincoln – the line usually runs down the block for weekend brunch.

hats squeeze in to devour smokey brisket burritos, crispy hash browns, and pancakes made with Fruity Pebble cereal – all washed down with a reviving Bloody Mary.

MIKE'S CITY DINER

Map 2; 1714 Washington Street, South End; ///live.carbon.salads; www.mikescitydiner.com

When Jay Hajj opened this greasy-spoon joint in 1995, Washington Street was a bit down-at-heel. Times may have changed – the area is now the gateway to Boston's thriving arts district – but this old-school spot has retained its no-frills vibes. Expect huge, great-value portions of classic diner fare (all made from scratch) and super-retro decor; oh, and it's cash only. The crowd is a varied bunch: think construction workers, students on a budget, and doctors just off the night shift.

FRENCHIE

Map 2; 560 Tremont Street, South End; ///jams.cards.bared; www.frenchieboston.com

Want to impress your brunch date? With its bouquet-topped tables and moody lighting, this darling little French restaurant has major modern-romantic vibes. Be warned, though, your one true love might actually be the bechamel-kissed mushroom buckwheat crêpe – it's truly one in a million.

» Don't leave without grabbing a table in the glass-walled solarium in the back; it's intimate, ultra-cozy, and decorated with fairy lights.

Solo, Pair, Crowd

Rolling solo? Eating with your brunch bunch? Whatever the crowd, Boston has you covered.

FLYING SOLO

Waffles for one

Solo brunchers don't need to line up at The Friendly Toast. Instead, head straight to the bar and get an order in for a stack of waffles or pancakes. You'll leave feeling full and just a little bit smug.

IN A PAIR

Shakshuka to share

Take your best bud for a brunch date at Milkweed, a cute corner café in Mission Hill. Order a shakshuka to split, then finish off with some dutch baby pancakes topped with creamy lemon ricotta.

FOR A CROWD

Pancakes for all

Bootleg Special is an airy, New Orleans-inspired joint that's perfect for groups. Come for the signature, immensely shareable seafood boils and stay for the (equally shareable) fluffy soufflé pancakes.

COMMITTEE

Map 5; 50 Northern Avenue, Seaport; ///gravel.entertainer.march;
www.committeeboston.com

With its industrial-chic vibes (complete with concrete floors and glowing filament bulbs), this swanky Seaport spot attracts a bougie crowd. Creative Greek plates are the name of the game, perhaps hefty breakfast gyros or feta-filled *sfougato* (a type of frittata).

STILLWATER

Map 2; 120 Kingston Street, Downtown; ///stay.precautions.luxury;
www.stillwaterboston.com

It's best to wear your stretchiest pants to Stillwater – this is where brunch goes big. It's no surprise, really, since chef/owner Sarah Wade is a bona fide gourmet junk-food expert. Expect huge breakfast sandos on Texas toast and biscuits slathered in gravy.

» Don't leave without grabbing a side of "liquid gold" cheese sauce to douse indulgently all over your food.

MIKE AND PATTY'S

Map 2; 12 Church Street, South End; ///song.vocab.exists;
www.mikeandpattys.com

For breakfast on the go, look no farther than Mike and Patty's. This small-but-mighty café boasts some of the best brekkie sandwiches in town, made-to-order by friendly staff and served to-go in a paper bag. Try the vegan option with mushroom hash or indulge in the "grilled crack" sandwich with extra bacon and four kinds of cheese.

Delicious Seafood

Thanks to its coastal location, Boston's seafood is always super-fresh and plentiful. It's little wonder, then, that it's at the heart of the city's foodie scene, from grilled oysters to lobster-topped waffles.

THE PEARL

Map 5; 20b District Avenue, Dorchester; ///stone.vague.ends; www.thepearlsouthbay.com

You wouldn't expect to find one of the city's best seafood restaurants right in the middle of an outdoor shopping mall, but The Pearl is full of surprises. The brainchild of a group of childhood friends, who wanted to celebrate their family seafood recipes, this sleek space is all about welcoming vibes, great music, and lots of laughter. Head

Try it!
AW-SHUCKS

Take one of East Boston Oysters' *(www.eastbostonoysters.com)* pop-up shucking classes. You'll learn how to shuck and serve the tricky bivalves, and leave the class with your very own shucking knife.

here with your own buds and break bread with shareables like fried calamari, bacon-wrapped scallops, and crab cakes. Maybe keep the chargrilled oysters (a dish you'll find nowhere else in Boston) to yourself, though. They're just too good.

IVORY PEARL
Map 6; 1704 Beacon Street, Brookline; ///move.handed.food; www.ivorypearlbar.com

Katsu and caviar might sound a little zany, but trust us, it's delicious. Ran Duan, Ivory Pearl's owner, is famous for pushing boundaries and he'll get you on side in no time. Give the African peri-peri fish fry a try, or opt for the rather posh-sounding caviar tater tots – you really can't go wrong with anything here, though.

» **Don't leave without** planning to come back for the oyster happy hour (5–6pm every day), where these little beauties are half price.

JAMES HOOK & CO.
Map 1; 440 Atlantic Avenue, Seaport; ///task.admiral.swift; www.jameshooklobster.com

Seaport may have gotten a shiny new makeover, with glittering skyscrapers replacing old warehouses, but James Hook stands as a reminder of the neighborhood's past. This unadorned counter-service spot (it's actually a double-wide trailer) has been knocking around for almost a century – and no wonder, with seafood this good. Join the line made up of steadfast loyalists and order the extra-thick clam chowder or top-notch lobster rolls doused in butter.

SELECT OYSTER

Map 3; 50 Gloucester Street, Back Bay; ///split.hobby.theme;
www.selectboston.com/select

Chef Michael Serpa loves New England seafood as much as the next Bostonian, but wanted to move beyond the usual dishes. So he opened this stylish restaurant to spotlight the region's ocean bounty a little differently. Okay, you won't get your "chowdah", but you'll be blown away by dishes like halibut topped with golden raisins and almonds, and Maine mussels braised in coconut milk.

NEPTUNE OYSTER

Map 1; 63 Salem Street, Suite 1, North End; ///hands.fame.chains;
www.neptuneoyster.com

Nestled amid the North End's many Italian eateries is this tiny but mighty oyster bar, which draws seafood lovers from all over the state. They don't come for its oysters, though (despite them being delicious). No, people descend on this diminutive spot for its 20-year-old calling card: hot butter lobster rolls. These massive treats are served on a toasted brioche bun – to help soak up all the extra butter, of course.

KAVA NEO-TAVERNA

Map 2; 315 Shawmut Avenue, South End; ///fits.actual.pump;
www.kavaneotaverna.com

So this place doesn't focus exclusively on seafood, but we had to include it here anyway. Found on a quiet street, this family-owned restaurant makes you feel like you're on the Greek coast, thanks to its salt-washed walls and knotted ropes, plus dishes like baked shrimp with feta and deep-fried sardines. It's perfect for a catch-up with a bestie thanks to the free-flowing Greek wines, and, in true Mediterranean style, you can linger for hours without stink eye from management.

B & G OYSTERS

Map 2; 550 Tremont Street, South End ///sweat.pound.simple;
www.bandgoysters.com

Barbara Lynch is a local legend. The one-time pal of famed TV cook Julia Child has won many an award, including the title of R&C Grand Chef (the only woman in North America to hold the title). Devotees of her cooking return over and over to one of her earliest restaurants: this tiny oyster bar, tucked away in the South End. It's *the* place to sample seared scallops and whole branzino.

SALTIE GIRL

Map 2; 279 Dartmouth Street, Back Bay; ///marked.breath.await;
www.saltiegirl.com

It was early childhood memories of sailing around New England with her dad that sparked Kathy Sidell to open this restaurant. There's everything here from huge lobster rolls to torched salmon belly, but our hands-down favorite is the fried lobster and waffles. It might sound weird, but this sweet-and-salty combo is the delicious indulgence you never knew you needed.

» Don't leave without sampling something from the extensive tinned seafood collection, inspired by Kathy's travels around Europe.

Sandos and Quick Bites

Bostonians are busy folks – they work hard, play hard, and often need to grab food on the run. Luckily, the city has countless places that can whip up a sando (that's a sandwich to me and you) or light bite in minutes.

LIFE ALIVE

Map 4; 765 Massachusetts Avenue, Cambridge; ///dare.scuba.oven; www.lifealive.com

Think fast food can't be healthy? Think again. Decorated with bright textiles and mandala motifs, this yogi-style café serves up super-wholesome, organic veggie fare to-go. We'll take the colorful Buddha bowl and a turmeric latte, thanks.

CUTTY'S

Map 3; 284 Washington Street, Brookline; ///lies.arts.dusty; www.cuttyfoods.com

Laid-back Cutty's is run by Rachel and Charles Kelsey, a husband-and-wife team who set out to make the perfect sandwich. And oh my, did they succeed, thanks to a perfectly balanced ratio of fresh fillings to handmade crusty bread. Our pick? The Rabe T.J., a delicious mix of bitter broccoli rabe, mozzarella, and melty provolone, squished between two toasted sesame-seed buns. Yum.

ANOUSH'ELLA

Map 2; 35 W Newton Street, South End; ///patio.dots.jacket; www.anoushella.com

Taught to cook by her Armenian mother while growing up in Lebanon, Nina Festekjian later fine-tuned her skills through rustling up recipes for her three sons. Today, at this sleek, fast-casual spot, she serves Lebanese Armenian dishes that pay homage to her heritage. The shining stars are the paper-thin m'anoush wraps, which envelop the most flavorful fillings: think tender pulls of za'atar-cloaked chicken, herbaceous salads, and silken hummus.

>> **Don't leave without** nabbing a tub of the excellent walnut harissa to dollop atop eggs or dunk pita triangles once you're home.

CHILACATES

Map 2; 275 Shawmut Avenue, South End; ///finely.note.weedy; www.chilacatesmx.com

In a city not known for quality Mexican cuisine, Chilacates is a beacon of burrito-y goodness. South End locals pop by this cozy space (decorated with a colorful mural of Frida Kahlo, the unofficial patron saint of Mexico) to pick up a freshly made corn tortilla packed with one of ten tasty fillings. Too hungry to take-out? Grab one of the coveted stools inside and nosh away.

SHIRLEY

Map 4; 22A College Avenue, Somerville; ///often.chats.lakes;
https://shirleyeatmoresunshine.square.site

Kat Bayle named this little bakery after her grandmother, Shirley, who taught her the benefits of fresh, locally sourced, and seasonal food. This principle runs through all the items on the menu, from the famed tofu banh mi to the delicious cinnamon toast with fruit butter.

MAMALEH'S

Map 4; 15 Hampshire Street, Cambridge; ///occupy.unit.chin;
www.mamalehs.com

This modern-day Jewish deli offers a dose of comfort and retro whimsy in tech-hub Kendall Square, with its penny-tiled bar and frosted light fixtures. Start-up workers and students come to devour dishes winking at the traditional, like hefty Reubens (grilled sandwiches bursting with

Shh!

Don't be fooled by the modest facade of this humble convenience store, which is marked by a simple black-and-white sign. P & K Delicatessen *(www.pkdeli somerville.wixsite.com)* actually serves up some of Boston's best sandwiches. Sure, the Italian sub (generously jam-packed with cured meats and cheese) generates a bit of a buzz. But neighborhood residents know the real star of the show is the deli's liberally sauced, but never soggy, meatball sub. Grab a napkin and enjoy.

corned beef, sauerkraut, Swiss cheese, and Russian dressing) and matzah ball soup. After something sweet? Try a fudgy chocolate babka good enough to rival bubbe's (sorry, grandma).

» **Don't leave without** a bag of homemade bagels and schmear to-go, and maybe a jar of amazing pickle salt, too.

MONICA'S MERCATO
Map 1; 130 Salem Street, North End; ///crew.gosh.cans; www.monicasnorthend.com

Set up by three brothers, this deli-market is one of the few places in the North End where longtime locals and trendy newcomers coexist in harmony. You can attribute that to the shop's carefully crafted, made-to-order subs (bread rolls filled with meat, cheese, and veggies), especially the absolutely bomb Italian option. This drool-worthy masterpiece of thinly sliced meat is perfection.

PINK CARROT
Map 1; 115 Salem Street, North End; ///finds.hosts.afford; www.pinkcarrotboston.com

Sat among the carb-rich Italian joints of the North End, Pink Carrot is all about healthy, comforting food. Digital nomads post up here for the day with their laptops, sipping on expertly crafted coffee, while lunchtime joggers pop in for a fresh, filling salad. If you're in a hurry, nab one of the stuffed sweet potatoes – especially the one topped with chocolate chips, banana slices, and a generous smear of peanut butter. It'll keep you going for hours, promise.

Comfort Food

Let's face it – Boston's winter weather can be a bit of a drag. Happily, the howling wind and icy streets have inspired local chefs to craft rich, indulgent food that will warm you to your very bones.

SANTARPIO'S

Map 6; 111 Chelsea Street, East Boston; ///spoil.rating.foods; www.santarpiospizza.com

Who serves the city's best slice is a source of heated debate among Bostonians, but we say it's Santarpio's. At this no-frills pizzeria, the Santarpio family has been slinging up incredible pies for hungry Eastie punters since 1933. What makes them so good? Well, this spot adds the toppings to its ultra-thin crunchy crust before sprinkling generously with cheese – it helps give an extra punch of flavor.

VEGGIE GALAXY

Map 4; 450 Massachusetts Avenue, Cambridge; ///photo.opens.invite; www.veggiegalaxy.com

With its vintage space-age vibes, this place offers all of the nostalgia of an old-school, all-American diner – but with a twist. Every item on its menu is 100 percent vegetarian and can be made vegan on request. That doesn't mean the food skimps on tummy-filling goodness, though: here, you'll find eager locals devouring heaped helpings of fiery Nashville hot chick'n and the world's gooiest loaded nachos. Wear your loosest pants.

» **Don't leave without** slurping one of the rich and foamy milk-free frappes (we vote for the decadent peanut butter chocolate).

MEI MEI

Map 5; 58 Old Colony Avenue, South Boston; ///pure.first.camps;
www.meimeiboston.com

Feeling dumpling deficient? Head to cute café Mei Mei at the Iron Works South Boston. The brewery-style joint is run by chef Irene Li and her two siblings, who started dishing out dumplings as a way to celebrate their Chinese American roots. Their crowning glory is the wonderfully unconventional cheddar scallion potato, filled with (as the name suggests) a mouthwatering mix of creamy potatoes, super-cheesy cheddar, and peppery scallions. Dreamy.

Try it!
A DUMPLING DATE

There's no better place to hone
your dumpling-making skills than at one
of Mei Mei's workshops. The two-hour
sessions cover all sorts of skills, ranging
from pan-searing to hand-folding.

TONY AND ELAINE'S

Map 1; 111 N Washington Street, North End; ///grades.long.tricks;
www.tonyandelaines.com

Pop by this kitschy trattoria any night of the week to find extended Italian families noshing on classics like baked gnocchi and piping-hot mozz sticks. All the dishes here are great, but you can't go wrong with the award-winning meatballs.

» Don't leave without scrolling the restaurant's socials, which showcase owner Tony's amazingly deadpan sense of humor.

SULLIVAN'S

Map 6; 2080 William J. Day Boulevard, South Boston;
///solve.quiz.deeply; www.sullivanscastleisland.com

Come spring, folks from across Boston line up at this family-run seafood shack to grab its ketchup-loaded hot dog and crinkle-cut fries combo. It's a match made in heaven, which might be why this menu stalwart has remained unchanged since the 1950s.

EL PEÑOL

Map 6; 54 Bennington Street, East Boston; ///roses.pads.offers;
www.elpenolrestaurant.com

Two decades ago, Doña Marina Balbín left Colombia to open this unassuming restaurant in East Boston. Since then, it's been a hub for homesick Colombians and beyond, thanks to its comforting dishes. Try the *bandeja paisa* (a king-size plate of carne asada, beans, and sweet plantain) or warming tripe-loaded stew *sopa de mondongo*.

Liked by the locals

"Boston is jam-packed with stick-to-your-ribs delights. You'll find everything from hearty Italian fare in the North End to delicious Colombian dishes in East Boston – and that's just the tip of the iceberg. It's the perfect place to dig in."

RACHEL BLUMENTHAL,
EDITOR OF BOSTON MAGAZINE

Sweet Treats

*This is the birthplace of marshmallow fluff,
the iconic Boston cream pie, and, of course, Dunkin'
and its famed donuts. Join locals indulging their
sweet tooth at one of these top-notch places.*

FOMU

**Map 2; 655 Tremont Street, South End; ///then.mutual.logo;
www.fomuicecream.com**

Feel good about indulging your sweet tooth at this sustainable ice
cream parlor, which serves up deliciously velvety scoops. Everything
is vegan, made without artificial ingredients, and has all sorts of
local, seasonal goodies mixed in. Oh, and FoMu uses eco-friendly
packaging, too. No wonder there's always a line here (even in the
depths of winter).

FLOUR

**Map 2; 1595 Washington Street, South End; ///record.regime.unwanted;
www.flourbakery.com**

Mention Flour to any Bostonian and you'll be met with a wistful sigh,
followed by "oh those sticky buns." Made by award-winning pastry
chef Joanne Chang, these soft brioche buns – drizzled with caramel

It pays to get to Flour on the early side (the store opens at 7am), as the good stuff sells out really quickly.

and toasted pecans – are the stuff of legend. Once you've grabbled one to-go, find a bench in nearby Peters Park and devour the sticky sweet treat with glee.

MODERN PASTRY

Map 1; 257 Hanover Street, North End; ///epic.view.gravel; www.modernpastry.com

You can't throw a stone in the North End without hitting a bakery serving cannolis, but Modern is the best. Despite the name, this retro store (it's cash only) is one of the OGs, having been owned by the same family for over 80 years. Each crispy cannoli shell is hand-filled to order with airy ricotta that has just the right amount of sweetness.

>> **Don't leave without** grabbing a drink at the secret bar downstairs, which specializes in sweet martinis, including a pistachio-flavored one.

MIKE'S PASTRY

Map 1; 300 Hanover Street, North End; ///blunt.life.tone; www.mikespastry.com

So when we said Modern has the best cannolis, we forgot to mention that there's some gentle (read: fierce) debate among locals on this topic. In fact, many Bostonians say Mike's (which was set up back in 1946) is the clear winner. Its decadent cannolis are massive, coming in flavors like Oreo and limoncello, and liberally sprinkled on both ends with chocolate chips, hazelnuts, or almonds. Mike's is just down the street from Modern, so why not hit up both and decide for yourself?

Solo, Pair, Crowd

From treats for one to sweets to share, Boston's got all of your sugar cravings covered.

FLYING SOLO
Mousse for moi
Somerville's tiny Gâté Comme des Filles serves up luxurious chocolate mousse in a cone (among other chocolatey delights). Grab one to-go and explore the other small independent shops at artsy Bow Market.

IN A PAIR
Rosewater romance
Grab a table for two on the small patio of Sofra, a bakery serving Turkish and Middle Eastern-influenced treats. Order one slice of the almond rose cake, one of the chocolate tahini tart, and get sharing.

FOR A CROWD
English muffins all round
There's no risk of food envy between you and your friends at Vinal Bakery. That's because you'll all be getting the same thing: the bakery's chewy housemade English muffins, slathered generously with jam.

BLACKBIRD DONUTS

**Map 2; 492 Tremont Street, South End; ///bids.float.sector;
www.blackbirddoughnuts.com**

It's not just Dunkin' *(p82)* that makes a good donut. South End locals love this chic little spot, which is known for its melt-in-your-mouth, just-sweet-enough offerings. Step inside the black-and-pink space to pick your fave, whether it's salted toffee, chocolate sprinkle, or the "Boston Cream" (filled with vanilla bean custard and encased in chocolate ganache). Here on a summer day? Make your donut into an ice-cream sandwich with help from the shop's silky soft serve.

» Don't leave without snagging the popular "everything bagel" donut. Made of pillowy brioche dough, it's filled inside with cream cheese and topped with onion, garlic, and sesame and poppy seeds.

TATTE

**Map 2; 399 Boylston Street, Back Bay; ///lime.crisis.types;
www.tattebakery.com**

Despite its chic Parisian-esque digs, this French-style patisserie has humble roots. When its founder Tzurit Or moved to the US from Israel, she began baking from her kitchen as a way to help her feel at home in a new place. She first sold her creations at Copley Square farmers' market, and they were such a success that she set up a brick-and-mortar café in 2008 – then another, and another. Today, Tatte has 22 outposts in Boston, with this little jewel in Back Bay one of the best. Between subway-tiled walls crowds devour dreamy pecan tarts, mini cheesecakes, and tender slices of pear pie, each created with classic French patisserie techniques and Israeli flair.

Special Occasion

Toasting a birthday? Graduation? Or another Red Sox win? When celebrations are in order, locals make for these special spots. There's no need to dress up, though, as Bostonians are a pretty casual lot.

CELESTE

Map 4; 21 Bow Street, Somerville; ///rates.owner.laser;
www.celesteunionsquare.com

Celeste is great for a casual birthday bash. At this pint-size place, the flower-filled dining room looks straight into the kitchen, giving the space laid-back dinner party vibes. Flavorful Peruvian food abounds, all slinged up by Peru-born head chef Juanma Calderón. Try *causas* (seafood-filled potato dumplings) or tuck into the Indigenous dish *carapulcra* (savory pork stew with peanuts and potatoes).

O YA

Map 2; 9 East Street, Downtown; ///tilt.laptop.trails; www.o-ya.restaurant

At this swanky, low-lit Japanese joint, you'll find couples honoring anniversaries and close friends toasting big birthdays. Those looking to treat themselves should go for the 20-course *omakase* dinner: it's a feast for the eyes and the stomach, complete with decadent ingredients like yuzu truffle and white sturgeon caviar. Full disclosure: prices run pretty steep here, but with food this good, you'll be justified in pushing the boat out.

MISTRAL

Map 2; 223 Columbus Avenue, Back Bay; ///form.twin.again; www.mistralbistro.com

This French restaurant brings some serious flair to the table: expect elegant white tablecloths, high ceilings, and massive floor-to-ceiling windows that wouldn't look out of place in a Provençal château. It's popular with local high rollers, who come to dine on roasted duck, escargots, and other decadent French fare. It's the perfect place to take your parents or in-laws when they're in town – we guarantee they'll be talking about your excellent taste for years to come.

OLEANA

Map 4; 134 Hampshire Street, Cambridge; ///potato.strain.gates; www.oleanarestaurant.com

Following a couple of trips to Turkey, Seattle-born Ana Sortun set up this polished Cambridge spot. While the Middle Eastern dishes might be inspired by cuisines across the Atlantic, the ingredients are local. In fact, most are sourced from her husband's farm, an hour or so from the city. Grab a seat on the gorgeous outdoor patio and celebrate your special occasion with spinach falafel or lamb kofte.

» Don't leave without trying one of Oleana's inspired desserts, like the meringue-cloaked, caramel-drizzled baked Alaska.

PAMMY'S

Map 4; 928 Massachusetts Avenue, Cambridge; ///gaps.chop.scare;
www.pammyscambridge.com

Nestled between Harvard and Central Square, this ultra-cozy
trattoria is the perfect place for a romantic rendezvous. First-date
jitters melt away beneath the warm glow of the globe lights, with
the food (involving new takes on Italian American grub, like homey
bolognese with Korean *gochujang*) sure to impress. There's even
a roaring fireplace – what more do you need?

ALDEN & HARLOW

Map 4; 140 Brattle Street, Cambridge; ///salad.looks.chose;
www.aldenharlow.com

Inspired by homecooked dinners with his family, chef Michael Scelfo
wanted to bring folks together over food, so he set up this laid-back
joint. The menu here focuses on small plates, which are devoured at

Shh!

On shoppers' paradise Newbury
Street, Faccia a Faccia *(www.
facciaafacciaboston.com)* isn't
all that under the radar, it's true.
But only locals know that this
is the one place in the city that
crafts handmade gluten-free

pasta in spades. It's a stylish
spot, too, with whitewashed
brick walls and elegant walnut
chairs, making it a great place
to treat your best buddy to a
birthday meal of squid ink
trottole or seafood *paccheri*.

the long wooden tables, making for a super-sociable feast. Needless to say, it's the perfect place to reunite the gang: order the pickled corn pancakes and chicken-fried rabbit (two of the restaurant's most-loved dishes) and get sharing.

MIDA

Map 3; 782 Tremont Street, South End ///oasis.busy.merit; www.midarestaurant.com/mida-boston

This buzzy South End eatery is proficient in all things pasta, treating hungry punters to decadent rock shrimp carbonara and hearty ricotta manicotti – plus a whole laundry list of other carb bombs. Drop by for a pay-day treat with your workmates: the large windows and open kitchen make it a good shout for a round of post-work people-watching.

» Don't leave without bookmarking the Mangia Monday deal. This menu-for-two includes five decadent pasta entrées.

FIELD & VINE

Map 4; 9 Sanborn Court, Somerville; ///tolls.count.hurt; www.fieldandvinesomerville.com

It's all about sustainable farming and locally sourced produce at Field & Vine, with seafood, greens, and even wine and beer chosen with the environment in mind. The light-filled interior is stunning: leafy green plants cluster around a big window, while an artistic array of branches and dried flowers, strung with fairy lights, hangs from the ceiling. It makes a beautiful setting for your celebration.

An afternoon in
Boston's Little Italy

The city's North End has been a hub for all things Italian since the 1860s, when immigrants first came to the area. Many new arrivals set up restaurants, cafés, and delis selling everything from tempting Sicilian cannoli to Neapolitan pizza – flavors that reminded the growing community of home. Today, this patch remains both the stomping ground of long-standing locals and a hot spot for delicious Italian eats. Spend some time here sampling – just remember to wear your loosest pants.

NORTH WASHINGTON STREET

THACHER STREET

ENDICOTT STREET

*In August, **St. Anthony's Feast** sees North End's streets come alive with parades, music, and food stalls selling arancini, cannoli and gelato.*

1. Modern Pastry
257 Hanover Street, North End; www.modernpastry.com
///epic.view.gravel

2. Salumeria Italiana
151 Richmond Street, North End; www.salumeria italiana.com
///club.forces.wage

3. Caffé Vittoria
290–296 Hanover Street, North End; www.caffe vittoria.com
///stir.smiled.origin

4. I AM Books
124 Salem Street, North End; www.iambooksboston.com
///fishery.modest.salad

5. Regina Pizzeria
11 ½ Thacher Street, North End; www.reginapizzeria.com
///ranges.farms.major

6. Parla
230 Hanover Street, North End; www.parlaboston.com;
///linen.forces.grass

St. Anthony's Feast
///paying.sheet.tidy

Defilippo
Playground

0 meters 100
0 yards 100

NORTH
END

SALEM STREET

Paul
Revere
Mall

PRINCE

THACHER ST

STREET

STREET

HANOVER

**Browse the shelves at
I AM BOOKS**

Check out the enviable
collection of Italian cookbooks
at this cute bookstore, which
specializes in works by Italian
and Italian American authors.

NORTH MARGIN STREET

5 **Grab a slice at
REGINA PIZZERIA**

At this beloved spot, devour
some of Boston's best pizza
slices (think a pillowy crust
and ample cheese).

4

PRINCE STREET

COOPER STREET

SALEM STREET

PARMENTER STREET

HANOVER STREET

3 **Espresso time at
CAFFÉ VITTORIA**

Time for a pick-me-up at
Boston's oldest Italian café.
Fancy something sweet?
It also serves the silkiest
scoops of gelato. Just saying.

**Fuel up at
MODERN PASTRY**

Start your foodie odyssey
here, where top-notch ricotta
cannoli are filled fresh to order.

1

2

**Pick up provisions at
SALUMERIA ITALIANA**

Over 40 years ago, Erminio and
Vanda Martignetti set up this
Italian market to give their son
a taste of their native Italy (he
still owns the place, by the way).

6

**End your tour at
PARLA**

Sip on a drink at this
speakeasy-style cocktail
joint. If you're still hungry,
there are tasty Italian
small plates to graze on.

CROSS STREET

Rose Kennedy
Greenway

DRINK

Cafés and bars are key to Boston's local scene. Natural wines accompany debates with friends, coffees fuel study sessions, and beers are raised at sports bars and breweries.

Dives and Pubs

*Gathering in shabby dives and (slightly classier)
pubs to crush a few beers is a Boston tradition.
The city has lost a few stalwarts in recent years,
but those that remain are the real deal.*

BIDDY EARLY'S
**Map 1; 141 Pearl Street, Financial District; ///joke.home.stress;
www.biddyearlysboston.com**

The self-proclaimed "best damn dive in Boston" has all the marks of
a true dive: cheap drinks, dusty floors, and an ancient jukebox
tucked away in the corner. Drop by to sink a couple of beers, and to
rub shoulders with Biddy's cohort of disparate regulars, including
townies and finance bros – everyone's welcome here.

BELL IN HAND TAVERN
**Map 1; 45 Union Street, Downtown; ///luxury.digits.shut;
www.bellinhand.com**

A night at the Bell in Hand is a rite of passage for Bostonians –
slinging brews since 1795, it's the oldest operating pub in the city.
And though it may be getting on, it certainly doesn't lack life. Come
the weekend, its two floors are filled with the sounds of music. Live

Get to the Bell in Hand Tavern before 9pm on weekend nights to beat the cover charge.

bands take over the downstairs, while upstairs, DJs spin beats till the early hours. Topping it all off? An excellent selection of beers and cider on tap, of course.

THE SEVENS ALE HOUSE

Map 1; 77 Charles Street, Beacon Hill; ///mime.gifts.rails; 617-523-9074

This little shoebox of a dive shouldn't work. After all, it's found in the upper-crust Beacon Hill area, a place known more for its fashionable boutiques than its grungy dives. But somehow it keeps going strong – even after five decades. Why? It's got to be down to its loyal regulars, a friendly bunch who are happy shooting the breeze or challenging newcomers to a round of darts. Come and try your luck.

» Don't leave without ordering a Reuben sando, which comes piled with sliced corned beef and melty Swiss cheese.

THE DELUX

Map 2; 100 Chandler Street, South End; ///wicked.stuck.worm; www.thedelux.com

Locals were up in arms when this dive – one of the last bastions of the old South End – closed in 2014. Luckily, it wasn't shut for long, with husband-and-wife team Kyle and Laura, who had their very first date in Delux's funky digs, taking it on. They've barely changed a thing, staying true to the bar's wonderfully kitschy roots: think an Elvis-shaped lamp, wall collages of polaroids and vinyl sleeves, and year-round festive lights – oh, and a Christmas tree made from beer cans.

Solo, Pair, Crowd

The heart of Boston's bar scene, Irish pubs are just as welcoming to individuals as they are to a rowdy gang.

FLYING SOLO
Sláinte solo

Perch up at the bar in Sligo Pub, a classic Irish joint in Somerville. It's super-chill here, making it a great choice for a solo hang; no one will bother you if you need some peace with your beer.

IN A PAIR
Game night

Tucked in the city's Theater District, the Tam is decked out with Guinness flags and quirky arcade games. Indulge your competitive side and challenge your pal to a game or two.

FOR A CROWD
Rowdy crowd-y

Friends in town? Take them to the Plough and Stars in Cambridge. This local hangout is all about the entertainment, offering live music performances six nights a week and a trivia night on Mondays.

CHARLIE'S KITCHEN

Map 4; 10 Eliot Street, Cambridge; ///caves.normal.goes;
www.charlieskitchen.com

It doesn't take up much space in Harvard Square, but boy does Charlie's make its presence known. Every inch of its exterior is covered in neon signs, including one attempting to lure you in for a cheeseburger (heed this call). It doesn't stop there, though; inside there's even more neon, as well as strings of colorful lights crisscrossing the ceiling. Students have been ending their nights here for decades and today can often be found nursing some late-night suds at the bar. Those essays can wait, right?

» Don't leave without spending some time in Charlie's beer garden in the warmer months. Tucked away from the bustle of Harvard Square, it's a great place for a more chilled drink.

L STREET TAVERN

Map 5; 658 E 8th Street, South Boston; ///photos.rally.shirt;
www.woodyslstreet.com

Found in Boston's most Irish neighborhood, L Street has drawn considerable attention ever since it cameoed in the Oscar-winning movie *Good Will Hunting*. But it hasn't let cinematic fame go to its head. Remaining steadfastly down-to-earth, and run by lifelong Southie residents, it remains the stomping ground of old-school locals – folks who've lived here their whole life and remember the area before it became a party hangout for young professionals. Come here for St. Patrick's Day, when the beer flows freely, the music blasts, and South Bostonians old and new rub shoulders in harmony.

Wine Bars

It may not be the first thing that springs to mind, but wine bars are big in Boston. Mingle with fellow oenophiles at these cool, creative bars, sampling biodynamic wines or small-batch bottles.

DEAR ANNIE

Map 4; 1741 Massachusetts Avenue, Cambridge; ///pits.wins.budget; www.dearanniebar.com

The love child of two local wine experts, this pretty spot is all about small-production bottles and house-cured seafood. Draw up a chair at the long communal table, its surface decorated with flickering candles and seasonal blooms, and choose a wine from the ever-changing menu. Before you know it, you'll be sipping on a rare natural vino and making lifelong friends with the person next to you.

ZUZU'S PETALS

Map 4; 204 Hampshire Street, Cambridge; ///crisp.pipes.stops; www.zuzuspetalscambridge.com

This cute wine-and-dessert bar invites you to indulge in life's little luxuries *sans* cell phone. Here, any device with a screen is on the no-go list (you'll need to keep it in your bag). To be honest, though, once you've seen Zuzu's pick-your-own menu of sumptuous desserts and delicious European pours, you won't need any encouragement to stop scrolling. In fact, all you'll want to do is savor that Austrian reisling and tonka bean-infused crème brûlée for as long as possible.

REBEL REBEL

Map 4; 1 Bow Market Way, Somerville; ///manliness.tribe.clip; www.rebelrebelsomerville.com

Woman-owned Rebel Rebel offers natural wines with no nonsense – or "cool shit by the glass," as they put it. Friends squeeze into this tiny bar, sitting shoulder to shoulder as they make their selection from a list of offbeat vintages scrawled on a chalkboard above the bar. The focus is on the wine, so don't expect any pretentious small plates – just a bomb cheese board, potato chips, and olives.

» Don't leave without planning to brush up on your vino knowledge at one of the Wine School classes on Thursdays.

HALEY.HENRY

Map 1; 45 Province Street, Downtown; ///froze.drop.slot; www.haleyhenry.com

This woman- and LGBTQ+-owned bar is a stalwart of Boston's wine scene. Award-winning sommelier Haley Fortier runs the joint, which thrums with the conversations of its swanky, slightly edgy crowd. It's all about responsibly sourced, small-production wines here; oh, and there's tasty tinned seafood from Spain and Portugal to try as you sip a funky pet nat (sparkling wine) or crisp sauv blanc.

Liked by the locals

"Everywhere you look, people are talking about natural, sustainable, and responsibly sourced wine. It's a real vine-to-glass kind of movement and it's so refreshing to see."

HALEY FORTIER, OWNER OF
HALEY.HENRY AND NATHÁLIE

WINE BAR AT TASTING COUNTER

Map 4; 14 Tyler Street, Somerville; ///asserts.assist.noting;
www.tastingcounter.com

Eco-friendly restaurant Tasting Counter might be best known for its
high-end tasting menus, but it also has a more wallet-friendly wine
bar tucked away at its center. Drop by to sample sustainably produced
organic and biodynamic vintages (glasses start at just $8).

NATHÁLIE

Map 3; 186 Brookline Avenue, Fenway; ///codes.fast.agent;
www.nathaliebar.com

With its floral wallpaper and touches of gold, Nathálie stands apart –
and not only for its decor (as cute as it is). Sister bar to Haley.Henry
(p65), this romantic spot champions only natural, small production,
and women-made wines. Slide onto a banquette and get sipping.

THE KOJI CLUB

Map 6; 525 Western Avenue, Brighton; ///digs.ballots.goes;
www.thekojiclub.com

Okay, Koji Club isn't technically a wine bar, but its sommelier-
esque approach to all things sake means we had to include it.
Plus, this place is unique in Boston: it's the city's first and only sake
bar. Come to sample glasses of the traditional Japanese drink
(we love the sparkling sakes) alongside cool and curious patrons.
» Don't leave without sampling a limited-edition bottle, if you're
feeling flash (prices will likely hit a three-figure price tag).

Cocktail Joints

Sure, Boston has a reputation as a beer-loving city, but its cocktail scene is not to be sniffed at. Bartenders stir things up with some seriously creative concoctions, including offbeat takes on old classics.

SHOJO

Map 2; 9A Tyler Street, Chinatown; ///burns.darker.pocket;
www.shojoboston.com

Every night of the week Shojo is seemingly packed to the rafters. Why? Put simply, the cocktails are a league above. Here, East Asia ingredients are used to elevate classic cocktails: think baijiu-laden mules, Yakuza whiskey-based old fashioneds, and Vietnamese espresso martinis. Planning to visit on Friday or Saturday nights? You'll need to make a resy a couple of weeks in advance.

WIG SHOP

Map 1; 27 Temple Place, Downtown; ///metals.appear.abode;
www.wigshopboston.com

Hair of the dog has replaced actual hair at this wig-shop-turned-bar. From the outside, the joint still looks like a place to pick up a weave, what with a neon "wigs" sign and mannequin heads sporting old-school styles. Once you've stepped inside, though, it's a different story. Moody lighting and velvet booths give the place a 1960s supper club vibe except, instead of *Mad Men* types, it's filled with super-trendy customers flicking through a menu decorated with vintage wig ads.

» Don't leave without trying the Miami Nice, a mix of coconut-washed rum, strawberry Aperol, charred pineapple, and dry vermouth.

OFFSUIT

Map 2; 5 Utica Street, Leather District; ////raves.winter.device; www.offsuitboston.com

"Life's too short to drink boring shit." Offsuit's mantra gets right to the point, and likewise the concept here is straightforward. No password or dress code, just excellent cocktails and vinyl records played from start to finish on a turntable. The decor is library-meets-hunting lodge, with bookshelves, leather chairs, and glowing Tiffany lamps, plus a mounted deer head. It's undeniably cool, and without even trying – the coolest kind of cool.

Try it!
DISTILLERY TOUR

A cocktail is only as good as the spirits it's made with, and that's where Bully Boy Distillers comes in *(www.bullyboydistillers. com)*. Take a 45-minute tour of the distillery before sampling some of its rum and gin.

PARLA

Map 1; 230 Hanover Street, North End; ///linen.forces.grass;
www.parlaboston.com

You could order one of the many delicious drinks found on Parla's menu, but why play it safe? With the bar's Dungeon Master program, brave punters roll a 20-sided die to determine their order, leaving their cocktail fate in the lap of the mixology gods. It doesn't matter what you get, though – it's all creatively crafted and totally delicious.

FARMACIA

Map 1; 5 North Square, North End; ///span.easy.goal;
www.farmacianorthend.com

Diagnosis: cocktail boredom. Prescription: a visit to Farmacia. Housed in an old bootleg apothecary, this little nine-seat spot is super exclusive. You'll need to book a ticket (costing around $50) months in advance,

Tucked away down a modest little alley and hidden behind a plain black door marked only by a tiny gold logo, speakeasy-style Hecate (*www.hecatebar.com*) sure takes some finding. Once you're in, though, you won't want to leave. In this moody subterranean space – named after Hecate, the goddess of witchcraft – mystically inspired cocktails are served up on a black marble bar. The menu, which changes regularly, is decorated with cool and quirky illustrations.

but once you're inside the opulent space – complete with a gold-leaf ceiling and vintage marble bar – you'll be treated to three thought-provoking elixirs. Each one is conceived by owner and expert cocktail creator Philip Rolfe, who will quiz you on your drinking preferences before presenting you with the perfect panacea.

MARIEL

Map 1; 10 Post Office Square, Financial District; ///tape.rider.tubes; www.marielofficial.com

With its shuttered windows, tiled floor, and abundance of potted palms, Mariel could have been transported straight from mid-century Havana. A glammed-up crowd descends on this elegant space come evening to sip on minty mojitos, tequila-based cocktails, and beautifully crafted daiquiris, made with freshly squeezed juice and top-shelf rum.

PINE BAR

Map 1; 100 Hanover Street, Downtown; ///congratulations.combining.rainy; www.pinebarboston.com

Located inside the famed Boston Public Market, Pine Bar is all about keeping things local. The spirits here come from nearby distilleries, the syrups are handmade, and the garnishes are locally sourced. Even its name – based on the pine tree symbol on the New England flag – is regionally inspired. You can't get more Boston than that.

» Don't leave without trying one of the bar's regional brews before browsing the market for local produce.

Breweries

Bostonians might love to crush mainstream beers, but a good ol' Sam Adams isn't all they're after. Enter the city's craft breweries, which lure curious locals with everything from IPAs to sours.

NIGHT SHIFT BREWING

Map 1; 1 Lovejoy Wharf, Suite 101, West End; ///exit.birds.twig; www.nightshiftbrewing.com/locations/lovejoy-wharf

Back in 2007, three friends started homebrewing after work, often continuing their trials into the early hours – and it was worth the effort. Today, Night Shift (named after those late-night sessions) serves up some incredible brews, such as the hop-heavy Fluffy hazy (every IPA lover's fave). Bonus: it's located right next door to TD Garden, making it the perfect spot to toast a Bruins or Celtics victory.

LAMPLIGHTER BREWING CO.

Map 4; 284 Broadway, Cambridge; ///chip.others.curving; www.lamplighterbrewing.com

Flannel-donning craft beer nerds flock to Lamplighter for the juicy IPAs, but there's a lot more to this Broadway brewery than just the suds. Community is key here, with Tuesday Trivia, board game

Pub crawl? Pop by the Cambridge Brewing Company, just east of Lamplighter, for a diverse roster of brews. | nights, and NFL screenings packing the place out. There are even yoga classes – what better way to earn yourself a post-workout brew?

LORD HOBO CAMBRIDGE

Map 4; 92 Hampshire Street, Cambridge; ///string.unit.belong; www.lordhobo.com/cambridge

There's not a single craft beer fan in New England that hasn't heard of Lord Hobo. Your typical bearded and beanie-donning hipsters are on full display here, but the brewery's stellar reputation also draws folks from as far afield as Maine and NYC. Despite this celebrity, Lord Hobo keeps a relatively low-key profile: expect beat-up bar stools, classic comfort food, and TVs blaring whatever game is on.

>> **Don't leave without** trying flagship brew Boomsauce. Measuring in at 7.8 percent ABV, this double IPA is as dangerous as it is delicious.

TURTLE SWAMP BREWING

Map 5; 3377 Washington Street, Jamaica Plain; ///grant.wonderfully.pits; www.turtleswampbrewing.com

Jamaica Plain was once home to over 20 breweries, with Prohibition spelling doom for all but one (Sam Adams, of course). Today, Turtle Swamp serves as a modern-day love letter to JP's once-mighty beer scene. Grab an Orange Line (a citrusy New England IPA named after Boston's infamous fire-prone subway line), and take full advantage of the extensive board game selection.

Solo, Pair, Crowd

Whoever you're hanging with, find beers for you, two, or the whole crew at these Boston breweries.

FLYING SOLO
Beer and a show
Sam Adams Boston Taproom overlooks Dock Square, a popular place for street performers to congregate. Grab a seat on the rooftop patio and sip your brew while watching the show.

IN A PAIR
Sample some suds
Weird and wonderful beers abound at Trillium Brewing: think citrusy Berliner Weisse and chocolate peanut brittle stout. Come here for a tasting sesh and catch-up with your best bud.

FOR A CROWD
Take over a table
A long-standing New England beer giant, Harpoon Brewery is a great place to bring the gang. Commandeer one of the long communal tables in the industrial-chic beer hall and settle in for the evening.

DOWNEAST CIDER

Map 6; 256 Marginal Street, Building 32, East Boston;
///gown.windy.trying; www.downeastcider.com

Boston excels at hop-loaded DIPAs, but that doesn't mean the city can't get down with a little apple action, too. Over in Eastie, this waterfront warehouse dishes out a constantly rotating selection of house-brewed ciders, infused with some of the nation's finest fruits.

DISTRACTION BREWING CO.

Map 6; 2 Belgrade Avenue, Roslindale; ///cost.smart.ants;
www.distractionbrewingco.com

Brews can get a bit off-the-wall at this family-owned brewery. We're talking jalapeño-tinged pale ales, peach-infused witbiers, and crab-apple sours. After something more down-to-earth? No problem: there are also hazy NEIPAs and malty tripels (strong pale ales) on the menu.

AERONAUT BREWING COMPANY

Map 4; 14 Tyler Street, Somerville; ///verbs.pool.aside;
www.aeronautbrewing.com

There's no chance of boredom at Aeronaut. As well as arcade machines and board games, this light-strung brewery has a packed events calendar, including open mic sessions, indie trivia, and – best of all – Grateful Dead tribute nights. Snag one of the top-tier fruited sours or an IPA, and get ready to be entertained.

» Don't leave without exploring nearby Bow Market, a bustling place with more than 30 independent drinking, dining, and shopping spots.

Sports Bars

If there's one place that epitomizes the Boston bar scene, it's the humble sports bar. Here, fans gather to root ferociously for home teams like the Red Sox and the Bruins, all while knocking back a few cold ones.

STATS BAR & GRILLE

Map 5; 77 Dorchester Street, South Boston; ///boat.tamed.pouch; www.statsboston.com

Be prepared for a boisterous scene at this Southie spot – especially when the Celtics are shooting some hoops. On game day, dedicated fans donning green-and-white jerseys can be found staring at one of the bar's 24 flat screens, cheering wildly and sloshing their beers anytime the team scores a point. Get here early for any play-offs, as lines can quickly wrap around the corner.

BANNERS KITCHEN & TAP

Map 1; 82 Causeway Street, West End; ///traded.save.jobs; www.bannerskitchenandtap.com

This sprawling sports bar is the place to go if you don't want to miss a moment of the game. Here, a giant "Dream Screen" – an almost 40-ft- (12-m-) high projector screen – guarantees you'll catch all the action. Basketball fans drop in to shout on the Celtics, while Bruins diehards whoop as the players dash across the ice. If either are victorious, prepare for the atmosphere to get rowdy – especially when fans tumble in from nearby TD Garden to celebrate.

» **Don't leave without** booking you and your buddies in at the bar's Topgolf Swing Suites for a friendly game or two.

PARLOR SPORTS
Map 4; 1 Beacon Street, Somerville; ///crops.buddy.points; www.parlorsportsbar.com

Run by four passionate sports lovers, this pocket-size bar shelters all sorts of fans. Expect football play-offs featuring the New England Patriots (or Pats to fans), as well as Bruins showdowns, Celtics matchups, and even underloved US soccer matches. It's a friendly spot, so no matter what sort of sport has you cheering till you're hoarse, you're guaranteed to find some like-minded souls here.

THE BANSHEE
Map 5; 934 Dorchester Street, Dorchester; ///swift.spare.rails; www.bansheeboston.com

This Irish pub is a hub for expat European sports fans. In fact, it's not unusual to walk by and see a line of regulars – loyally draped in their team's scarves – already stretching out the door. International rugby and European soccer matches draw in punters, but the pub is also big on major league baseball (in typical Boston style). Grab a well-poured Guinness, crowd onto the sticky floor, and get ready to cheer.

THE MISSION BAR & GRILL

Map 3; 724 Huntington Avenue, Mission Hill; ///makes.charm.frogs;
www.themissionbar.com

Need sustenance to make it through a super-tense baseball game? Hotfoot it to this family-run bar for a piled-high burger and a crisp beer, and get ready to watch the play-by-play. Tip: find a seat by the giant streetside windows – if the Red Sox are losing, at least you can distract yourself with a bit of people-watching.

PHOENIX LANDING

Map 4; 512 Massachusetts Avenue, Cambridge; ///perky.gives.gather;
www.thephoenixlanding.com

Yes, you can watch the Red Sox or the Patriots at this classic Irish pub, but you won't be in the majority. This dimly lit bar is actually the official home of Boston's Liverpool fan club (yep, the English soccer team). Join ardent expats in bright red strips cheering on their

A sports bar masquerading as an Italian coffee shop, Caffe Dello Sport (www.caffedello sport.net) is a hidden hangout for soccer lovers and Celtics loyalists. The vibe is very different from your typical sports bar – there are no burgers and brews here, oh no. Instead, sip on high-quality espresso drinks and sweet cocktails (we can't get enough of the Nutella martinis) as you watch the game on the big screen.

beloved team from afar. And if Liverpool wins? Get ready to let loose with the regulars: the bar turns into a dance club come evening, with some of the city's best DJs spinning decks.

BLEACHER BAR

Map 3; 82A Lansdowne Street, Fenway; ///jumped.tulip.tennis; www.bleacherbarboston.com

Bleacher Bar is here for all those who haven't managed to get a Sox ticket. Tucked underneath the stands of Fenway Park, the space is decorated with old-timey baseball paraphernalia and, best of all, is fronted by glass doors so you're able to see the Sox (hopefully) flying around the bases. You'll find the usual jersey-clad devotees here, plus a handful of stunned tourists, who can't believe how loud Boston sports fans can get.

THE POINT

Map 1; 147 Hanover Street, Downtown; ///rising.prop.clocks; www.thepointboston.com

The Point is surprisingly laid back for a sports bar. Instead of the usual noisy spectators, you'll find a chill, slightly older crowd (so you might actually get to hear the game), clustering at the tables, nursing their drinks as they watch the action. There's delicious food, too; enjoy some clam chowder as the Celtics dribble their way to victory (fingers crossed).

» **Don't leave without** sampling a brew from the extensive menu, which includes seasonally rotating beers on tap.

Coffee Shops

Home to more indie cafés than you can shake a stick at, this is a city that runs on coffee. College students use endless espressos to fuel study sessions, while their professors debate big ideas over a flat white.

GREYSTONE

**Map 2; 123 Appleton Street, South End; ///hope.worker.hung;
www.greystonecafe.com**

Homemade pastries and aromatic coffees are the order of the day in this cute café, run by mother-and-daughter team Patty and Jaqueline. Inside the elegant farmhouse-inspired interior, you'll find South Enders enjoying lovingly crafted lattes and indulging in one of Patty's scrumptious cookies. In a rush? Grab your treats from the sidewalk take-out window, where locals wait in line with doggos and strollers in tow.

CICADA COFFEE BAR

**Map 4; 106 Prospect Street, Cambridge; ///rising.leave.native;
www.cicada.coffee.bar.square.site**

Jungle-like Cicada isn't the place to write that essay or catch up on work – it's a place to settle in and sip. Here, folks cozy up in one of the midcentury chairs or find a quiet nook in the garden out back, nursing Vietnamese coffees (including silky Sai Gon lattes made with condensed milk). The best thing? You can linger here all day. Come evening, Cicada transforms into a relaxed restaurant serving casual Vietnamese eats.

CAFFÉ VITTORIA

Map 1; 260–296 Hanover Street, North End; ///stir.smiled.origin; www.caffevittoria.com

An icon of Boston's Little Italy, this much-loved spot is the oldest Italian café in the city, having opened its doors way back in 1929. Step inside to join regulars drinking tiny macchiatos and cocoa-topped cappuccinos beneath the glistening tin ceiling, their effusive conversation occasionally drowned out by the whistle of the espresso machine. You might have dropped straight into a neighborhood café in Rome.

» Don't leave without grabbing some delicious gelato post-coffee; there's everything from pistachio to cookie dough flavors.

1369 COFFEEHOUSE

Map 4; 1369 Cambridge Street, Cambridge; ///canny.straw.answer; www.1369coffeehouse.com

This comfy neighborhood haunt has been bringing people together since the 1990s, thanks to its top-notch coffee and laid-back vibes. It's a big hangout hub for Cambridge's hippie-intellectual crowd, who pop by to catch up with friends, write that novel, or simply kick back with a book. Don't miss the community bulletin board; it's always popping off with the latest locals news.

GRACENOTE

Map 2; 108 Lincoln Street, Downtown; ///areas.king.windy;
www.gracenotecoffee.com

Gracenote proves that size doesn't matter when it comes to great coffee. This pint-size, plant-dotted café roasts its own beans in small batches nearby, meaning the coffee is always rich, aromatic, and super fresh. Pop into the light and bright space to try it for yourself – you won't be disappointed.

VESTER

Map 4; 73 Ames Street, Cambridge; ///epic.wage.chairs;
www.vestercafé.com

On a solo trip to Copenhagen back in 2014, Nicole Liu was inspired by the Danish capital's effortlessly chic and welcoming cafés. So when back on home soil, she set up the Nordic-inspired Vester. The coffee here is top-notch, but don't sleep on the food; Nicole comes

Shh!

In Boston, it feels like there's a Dunkin' on every street corner (*www.dunkindonuts.com*). This is no accident; locals run on coffees from the beloved donut shop. But it's only the most dedicated fans that make the pilgrimage to Dunkin's original store, found in Quincy, a suburb south of the city center. To avoid any raised eyebrows from the faithful, make like a regular and order your coffee iced – even in the dead of winter.

from culinary royalty (her mother pioneered Boston's first white-tablecloth Chinese restaurant in the 1980s). Our fave is the smørrebrød slathered with ricotta and topped with lingonberry.

HOME.STEAD

Map 5; 1448 Dorchester Avenue, Dorchester; ///riots.bring.yoga; www.dorchesterhomestead.com

Field's Corner is known for its Irish American pubs, Haitian restaurants, Vietnamese diners, and, last but certainly not least, coffee shop Home.Stead. This sweet little café is all about the community vibes. Not only does it host loads of events featuring local artists and musicians, and pays its staff fairly, it also supports the area's youngsters with training opportunities. To top it all off, the coffee and pastries are simply superb – what more is there to ask for?

JAHO COFFEE

Map 2; 665 Washington Street, Downtown; ///filled.risks.minus; www.jaho.com

Looking for a place to power through a project? Jaho is just the ticket. Beneath the café's wooden beams, chemistry-style equipment is used to whip up creative coffees, which keep remote workers going from morning into afternoon. Once the clock strikes 5pm, laptops are stuffed back into bags, the lights grow dim, and folk toast a successful day's work over a glass of beer or wine.

» **Don't leave without** trying the café's award-winning Scarlet Espresso Martini – it's perfect as a postwork pick-me-up.

An evening exploring
Boston's Irish pubs

Everyone knows that Bostonians *love* talking about their Irish heritage – this is the US's most Irish city, after all, with around 20 percent of the population claiming links with the Emerald Isle. Sure enough, this means that Boston is awash with traditional Irish pubs, with some of the best joints found in Downtown, just northeast of Southie, the heart of the city's Irish community. These welcoming watering holes offer Bostonians the perfect place to listen to lively music, nurse a pint of Guinness, and enjoy some great *craic*.

1. Emmets
6 Beacon Street, Downtown;
www.emmetsirishpuband
restaurant.com
///bucket.proper.builds

2. The Black Rose
160 State Street, Downtown;
www.blackroseboston.com
///soon.asserts.teach

3. Mr. Dooley's
77 Broad Street, Downtown;
www.mrdooleys.com
///held.maybe.forms

4. J.J. Foley's Cafe
117 E Berkeley Street,
South End; www.jjfoleys
cafe.com
///senior.cave.posed

📍 **Irish Heritage Trail**
///aware.event.total

CAMBRIDGE STREET

Grab a bite at
EMMETS
Begin your evening at Emmets; the food at this snug spot is just as good as the drinks it pours (we love the Guinness onion soup).

TREMONT STREET

STREET

WASHINGTON STREET

ESSEX STREET

CONGRESS STREET

STREET

CITY HALL
PLAZA

NORTH STREET

*Starting at the Rose
Kennedy Rose Garden,*
**The Irish Heritage
Trail** *charts the history
and heritage of Boston's
Irish population.*

Christopher
Columbus
Park

WATERFRONT

COURT STREET

STATE STREET

BROAD STREET

DOWNTOWN

CONGRESS STREET

WASHINGTON STREET

BATTERYMARCH

STREET

MILK STREET

**FINANCIAL
DISTRICT**

*Post Office
Square*

FRANKLIN STREET

STREET

PEARL STREET

CONGRESS STREET

STREET

STREET

OTIS STREET

PURCHASE

*Rose Kennedy
Greenway*

AVENUE

ATLANTIC

Catch a game at
THE BLACK ROSE

This pub's vintage tiles and
wooden bar are stunning.
Nab a booth and take it all
in as you sip on a brew.

Enjoy the music at
MR. DOOLEY'S

Enjoy some toe-tapping Irish
trad music at this proper
pub, where vintage posters
and pictures of notable
Irish folks adorn the walls.

Have a nightcap at
J.J. FOLEY'S CAFE

Round things off with a half
of stout at this pre-Prohibition
era bar. Family-owned for
over a century, this place is
a real Boston institution.

*Boston South
Station*

| 0 meters | 200 |
| 0 yards | 200 |

SHOP

Boston's free-thinking, creative spirit fuels its shopping scene. Browse for thought-provoking books, pick up handmade jewelry, or thrift for vintage threads.

Book Nooks

*Bostonians are a well-read bunch, so it makes sense
that the city is home to countless bookstores. Locals
love to spend their weekends browsing the shelves,
before hotfooting it home with a new read in hand.*

FRUGAL BOOKSTORE

Map 3; 57 Warren Street, Roxbury; ///ships.popped.once;
www.frugalbookstore.net

Leonard Egerton and Clarrissa Cropper are passionate about getting
books by Black writers into as many hands as possible – so they
founded Frugal. This welcoming community hub (Boston's only
Black-owned bookstore) is packed with an extensive range of
genres, including romance, and sci-fi. Plus, they keep their prices
affordable as a way to help promote literacy in the neighborhood.

WILD CHILD

Map 4; 1 Bow Market Way, Suite 32, Somerville;
///factories.plants.swept; www.wildchildsomerville.com

Love food? Love wine? Love books? Then Wild Child is for you.
A mix of cookbooks, food memoirs, and funky culinary zines lines
the shelves of this foodie-focused bookstore. Oh, and there's a bar,

Wild Child also hosts community-focused events, such as natural wine classes and food trivia nights. too, which serves pours by indie winemakers from underrepresented backgrounds. Have a browse, then kick back with a glass or two.

BEACON HILL BOOKS & CAFE

Map 1; 71 Charles Street, Beacon Hill; ///fees.define.flap; www.bhbooks.com

Spanning all five floors of a historic brick townhouse, this bookstore feels like the family home of your most stylish (and well-read) friend. In some rooms, bookshelves sit on either side of cozy fireplaces, while in others, comfy window seats invite you to lounge with a book plucked from a nearby shelf. There's even a cute kids' section, complete with a little model train that circles the room.

BRATTLE BOOKS

Map 1; 9 West Street, Downtown; ///stand.slam.small; www.brattlebookshop.com

When literary locals want to uncover secondhand treasures, they head to Brattle. One of the biggest (and oldest) used bookstores in the US, it's jam-packed with interesting reads. In fact, there are so many books here that they spill out onto the street; heaving stands are sandwiched into the alleyway beside the shop, tempting you to spend hours here perusing alfresco. Bring a tote bag to lug all your finds back home.

» Don't leave without chatting with owner Ken, who is more than happy to show you where the cool first edition titles lurk.

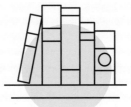

Liked by the locals

"All She Wrote is a place where
having conversations with people
is just as important as getting
them their next read. It is a safe,
inclusive space where you're loved,
cared for, and respected – no matter
what walk of life you come from."

CHRISTINA PASCUCCI CIAMPA,
OWNER OF ALL SHE WROTE BOOKS

ALL SHE WROTE BOOKS

Map 6; 451 Artisan Way, Somerville; ///deck.slang.twin;
www.allshewrotebooks.com

Book lover Christina created All She Wrote with one mission: to see books by women and other oppressed groups celebrated, rather than relegated to a single shelf. Pop by this warm hug of a store for the city's best collection of intersectional feminist and queer lit.

>> Don't leave without checking out the store's upcoming events, which include things like author talks and drag story hours.

MORE THAN WORDS

Map 2; 242 East Berkeley Street, South End; ///outer.grit.fake;
https://shop.mtwyouth.org

There are three reasons to love this nonprofit, secondhand bookstore. One: the well-stocked shelves. Two: the friendly, knowledgable staff. And three: the community focus, which includes supporting local teens who are homeless or in foster care by training them in the book biz.

PAPERCUTS J.P.

Map 5; 60 South Street, Jamaica Plain; ///dined.parents.deals;
www.papercutsjp.com

This store is tiny, but it sure packs a punch. Run by a former publishing professional, it's filled to the brim with a curated collection. Expect everything from famed classics to under-the-radar works and beyond – anything, really, that catches the team's expert eye. Join JP locals as they browse, looking out for the staff picks (they're always fab).

Record Stores

When it comes to music, Boston has produced some of the biggest names in the business. It's no surprise, then, that it's sprinkled with vinyl stores, stocking punk to pop and everything in between.

NUGGETS RECORDS

Map 3; 486 Commonwealth Avenue, Fenway; ///hands.senses.plans; www.nuggetsrecords.com

Channel your inner Cher and turn back time with a trip to this stalwart. A relic of the now-distant 1970s, Nuggets might be a bit dusty, a little underdecorated, and somewhat disorganized, but there's a goldmine of cassettes and CDs buried away if you're brave enough to get digging. Expect a pretty even spread of genres, spanning KISS to Boston's own Disco Queen, Donna Summer.

ARMAGEDDON SHOP

Map 4; 12 Eliot Street B, Cambridge; ///neck.pads.fingernails; www.armageddonshop.com

After a lengthy stint in hardcore punk band Dropdead, guitarist Ben Barnett decided to move into the world of vinyl, eventually setting up shop in Harvard Square. His record selection isn't restricted to his fave genre, though. A huge collection of records – covering the likes of industrial, garage, metal, and electronic – lures in a mix of inked-up rockers, long-haired metalheads, and dedicated punk fans. Best of all? The store has its own record label supporting local bands, so you might just find the next big name as you browse.

NEWBURY COMICS

Map 3; 348 Newbury Street, Back Bay; ///closer.driven.regime; www.newburycomics.com

First founded in the late 1970s by two MIT students, this store sells a real mishmash, from pop-culture paraphernalia to graphic novels. But it's the truly massive array of LPs, CDs, and cassettes that we're here for, with folk, reggae, bluegrass, and classical music all making an appearance. The store's amassed lots of swag over the years too, so watch out for limited-edition vinyl and autographed albums.

TRES GATOS

Map 5; 470 Centre Street, Jamaica Plain; ///curl.melon.liner; www.tresgatosjp.com

A trip to this record store and restaurant feels like popping around to a friend's place for dinner – if that friend had a wicked-good record collection, that is. Work up an appetite browsing the extensive, neatly ordered offerings, then stroll into the homey dining room for some tasty tapas.

» **Don't leave without** checking out Tres Gatos' excellent book selection – you're bound to find a post-dinner read on the packed shelves.

Solo, Pair, Crowd

Looking to browse alone or prefer to crate dig with a crew? Boston has a record store for you.

FLYING SOLO
Uncovering vintage vinyl

Time to treat yourself? Head to Vinyl Index, a vintage record store in Bow Market. It's a great place to rummage without any distractions — and you never know, you might finally uncover *that* old-school Aerosmith LP.

IN A PAIR
A musical afternoon for two

Somerville Grooves may be tiny, but it squeezes a king-size collection into its little space. Bring a fellow music-loving friend when you visit — you'll need a pal to help you carry all those records home.

FOR A CROWD
A diverse crowd

Take the crew to Cambridge's Cheapo Records, which hosts a huge collection of LPs, CDs, and cassettes. Plus, the genres are super diverse, so there's bound to be at least one record that everyone agrees on.

STEREO JACK'S RECORDS

Map 6; 736 Broadway, Somerville; ///guard.invent.kind;
www.stereojacks.com

Super-cool Somerville locals are in love with Stereo Jack's big
vinyl selection, especially since it's handily arranged in tidy rows
for quick flipping. Jazz is most certainly the main attraction, but
don't miss the classic rock, folk, or country albums either.

DEEP THOUGHTS JP

Map 5; 138b South Street, Jamaica Plain; ///flash.home.hunt;
www.deepthoughtsjp.com

It's all about obscure, off-the-wall deep cuts at this place, like
Japanese psych, krautrock, and synth waves. Step inside the kitschy
store (expect hanging baubles, Christmas lights, and dolls on the
walls) and let the super-friendly staff find you a new favorite record.
» Don't leave without checking out the store's live music schedule;
it hosts sessions by local acts and out-of-town performers alike.

PLANET RECORDS

Map 4; 144 Mount Auburn Street, Cambridge; ///liver.unique.pirate;
www.planet-records.com

Move over Destiny's Child – this certifiable survivor has made it
through remodels, floods, and even a fire. The Cambridge staple is
known for its curated CDs and LPs, with each item neatly sorted
into a designated row à la Boston Public Library. Keep an eye out
for the vintage band shirts and tour memorabilia, too.

Vintage Gems

*An eco-minded and thrifty lot, Bostonians are
big fans of secondhand gear. Locals love to dig
through the city's vintage stores, hoping to find
a preloved, one-of-a-kind piece.*

UPSTAIRS DOWNSTAIRS

Map 1; 69 Charles Street, Beacon Hill; ///major.enjoyable.museum;
www.upstairsdownstairsboston.com

Beacon Hill's antiques shops tend to be dusty, pricey, and, let's be
honest, not for everyone. But not Upstairs Downstairs. Run by the
ever-friendly Laura, this cheery treasure trove is packed with vintage
art pieces, table lamps, and barware – all at prices that won't break
the bank. Not sure what you're after? Laura will spend as much time
with you as you'd like to help pick something special.

BOOMERANGS

Map 5; 716 Centre Street, Jamaica Plain; ///chest.decreased.other;
www.shopboomerangs.org

Thrifty students looking to refresh their wardrobes for pennies on
the dollar hotfoot it to Boomerangs. This cavernous store is filled
with all the gently used threads your heart could desire. After a

Boomerang's South End outpost, meanwhile, is packed with designer brands, like Burberry and Celine. | stylish button down? You got it. Looking for a cute A-line skirt? It's here. And the best part? All proceeds support two local AIDS nonprofits.

RICK WALKER'S

Map 3; 306 Newbury Street, Back Bay; ///rear.lung.shins; www.rickwalkers.com

Visualize Mick Jagger as you strut on over to this Back Bay icon, which is still going strong at 85 years young. Inside, there's everything you need to dress like a rockstar (even if you can't sing like one), including vintage leather jackets, leather-print cowboy boots, and rare band tees. Watch out for famous musicians as you browse the rails: Ringo Starr has been known to pop by when visiting Boston.

SOWA VINTAGE MARKET

Map 2; 450 Harrison Avenue, South End; ///economies.crew.epic; www.sowavintagemkt.com

Vintage expert Stephanie Pernice established this indoor flea market over 10 years ago – and locals are super grateful she did. Come the weekend, savvy folks flock to the massive basement space to browse a smorgasbord of items from different vendors, including midcentury furniture, vintage clothing, and secondhand art. Oh, and the selection changes every week, so there's always a new gem to discover.

» Don't leave without seeking out Stephanie's golden retriever Emilie, who hangs out at her stall – he's a bit of a social media celeb.

BLUE BANDANA RELICS

Map 4; 1 Bow Market Way, Somerville; ///curry.dame.drums;
www.bowmarketsomerville.com/tenants/blue-bandana-relics

This snug man cave lures in creative gents with its cool "mantiques."
By this, owner Keith means secondhand Americana pieces like
cowboy hats and plaid shirts, as well as vintage sporting accessories
and home items. Have a rummage to uncover a funky find, like an
old-school NFL helmet or some antique barware.

THE GARMENT DISTRICT

Map 4; 200 Broadway, Kendall Square; ///spring.coherent.fund;
www.garmentdistrict.com

All hail the queen of Boston thrift stores: the Garment District. Locals
have been coming to this sprawling store for years, looking to spice up
their style with items from the extensive collection. Here, you'll find

What could be better than
browsing for vintage threads?
Doing that with a dose of
vintage games on the side,
of course. At High Energy
Vintage (www.highenergy
vintage.com), locals take a
break from scouring the rails
of secondhand clothes to
play a game of *Mr. Do!* on the
store's arcade machine. Want
to take some of the old-school
gamer vibes home with you?
There are also retro home
consoles from Nintendo and
Atari for sale.

the likes of sky-high 1960s go-go boots and early 2000s velour tracksuits (handily, all items are organized by decade). And come October, the place turns into Halloween central, with students and high schoolers hunting through the racks for the perfect costume.

» **Don't leave without** planning to pop by for the store's morning "by-the-pound" sales, where you pay two bucks for a pound of clothes.

40 SOUTH STREET
Map 5; 40 South Street, Jamaica Plain; ///mercy.stamp.august; www.fortysouthst.com

Hilken Mancini is a local rocker and all-around renaissance woman. Among other things, she's been the guitarist in four bands, produced a Green Day video, and created an inclusive punk rock-style aerobics workout. If that wasn't enough, she also runs this cool vintage shop that sells one-of-a-kind items. Expect a mix of 1950s tea dresses, 1980s boxy blazers, and – best of all – vintage band T-shirts depicting the likes of punk legends the Ramones or rock gods Van Halen.

CAMBRIDGE ANTIQUE MARKET
Map 4; 201 Monsignor O'Brien Highway, Lechmere; ///caring.lazy.crown; www.cambridgeantiquemarket.com

If you're looking for a little bit of everything, make for Cambridge Antique Market, an expansive spot blanketing five floors of an old industrial building. Just popping in for a browse? Be warned, you'll still probably end up leaving with an antique serving bowl, a couple of old-school beer steins, and a vintage action man.

Home Touches

*Long, cold winters spent indoors inevitably
leads to scrolling for home decor inspiration.
The good news? Boston has plenty of indie spots
to help turn design dreams into reality.*

HUDSON

**Map 2; 12 Union Park Street, South End; ///solo.vibrate.jukebox;
www.hudsoninteriordesigns.com**

Owned by local interior designer Jill Goldberg, this tiny shop
features a beautifully curated collection of New England-inspired
artisanal wares. Young South End moms looking for a slice of
coastal chic come here to pick up rattan tables, striped pillows,
and ocean-themed tea towels.

NICHE

**Map 4; 259 Elm Street, Davis Square; ///parts.pulse.beams;
www.nicheplantshop.com**

Every inch of this spacious shop is covered with plants. Tiny desktop
succulents cluster on the bright-white shelves, parlor palms and fruit
trees fight for room on the wooden floor, and sweetheart plants hang
from the ceiling. The staff are more like matchmakers than retailers:

after asking about your apartment and daily schedule, they'll attempt to pair you with the perfect houseplant – one that hopefully won't break up with you by dying two weeks later.

>> Don't leave without signing up for one of the store's "plant chats" sessions; each one covers a different topic on houseplant care.

ARTEFACT HOME

Map 2; 1317 Washington Street, South End; ///snail.carbon.daisy; www.artefacthome.com

Super-stylish architects and interior designers come to shop at this chic store in droves. The gorgeous items, many sourced from local designer-makers, are one-of-a-kind. Expect saddle-leather sofas, hand-carved gold wall mirrors, and elegant wooden coffee tables. The store also stocks plenty of affordable knickknacks that will fit into your tote, including divine charcoal soaps.

LEKKER HOME

Map 2; 38 Wareham Street, South End; ///tries.facing.buyers; www.lekkerhome.com

Natalie van Dijk, a Netherlands native, opened this store to introduce her adopted city to the design principles of Amsterdam, New York, and the like. Almost 20 years later, Lekker continues to lure in locals looking to jazz up their space with everything from extendable pine dining tables to sweet-smelling soy candles. Even better, Natalie is passionate about promoting small-batch makers from the US and beyond – all offering city sophistication, of course.

POD

Map 4; 35 Sacramento Street, Cambridge; ///final.cling.curve;
www.shop-pod.com

Want to add some flair to your digs? Pod can help. This petite corner store is packed with an eclectic mix of beautifully designed home items from around the world. Here, delicate Japanese porcelain pitchers share tables with glazed clay mugs from London, while plaid wool blankets from France nestle next to block-print coverlets from India.

CRANE AND TURTLE

Map 4; 1 Bow Market, Somerville; ///curry.dame.drums;
www.craneandturtle.shop

Welcome to the anti-IKEA: not a single item in this serene, silver-walled space is mass-produced. Instead, all the hand-picked home goods, many sourced from Japan, are durable and sustainably made – as well as being uniquely beautiful. We can't get enough of the delicate porcelain plates and gold-plated silverware.

» Don't leave without signing up for the store's *kintsugi* workshop, which is all about the Japanese art of repairing broken pottery.

SHAKE THE TREE GALLERY

Map 1; 67 Salem Street, North End; ///wire.rocket.camp;
www.shakethetreeboston.com

Three decades ago, Marian Klausner pivoted from practicing law to spotlighting the work of amazing local artisans. Her North End shop offers a little bit of everything: scented candles and cute little jugs dot the shelves, interspersed with colorful dresses, bouquets of dried flowers, and books dedicated to things like craft cocktails. Oh, and there's a beautifully curated selection of women's jewelry from local designers, too. Topping it all off, the store hosts regular shopping parties featuring up-and-coming makers from around the country (with cocktails and nibbles on the side, of course).

GRAYMIST STUDIO AND SHOP

Map 6; 364 Huron Avenue, Huron Village; ///vine.risky.crown; www.graymist.com

Back in 1995, Japanese-born Etsuko Yashiro visited Nantucket (a charming little island off the Massachusetts coast) for the first time and immediately fell in love with its aesthetic. So much so, in fact, that she set up this cute Cambridge store devoted to it. Pop by for nautical-inspired items: a boat-themed print, whale-shaped bookend, or a couple of bronze anchor wall hooks, perhaps. You can even learn how to make one of Nantucket's specialties (aka the rattan basket) at the classes led by Etsuko herself.

Try it!
CREATE WITH CLAY

Make something for your home at one of the Clay Lounge's pottery classes *(www. clayloungeboston.com)*, hosted in the artsy SoWa district. You'll learn the ways of the wheel and leave with two custom pieces.

Boston-Made Accessories

Lovingly stitched handbags, locally designed hats, and upcycled heirlooms: handmade accessories are big in Boston. Stop in at one of these cool stores to pick up a unique find from a local maker.

M. FLYNN

Map 2; 40 Waltham Street, South End; ///during.lost.prompting; www.mflynnjewelry.com

This chic jewelry store has a glam city apartment vibe, with its pretty pastel walls, glowing chandeliers, and vases of colorful blooms. Pop inside to browse a mix of super-cool pieces, from bright jelly hoop earrings to delicate gold bracelets.

STITCH AND TICKLE

Map 2; 63 Thayer Street, South End; ///small.moves.hurls; www.stitchandtickle.com

While working at Boston's Museum of Fine Arts, Sophie Truong got into sewing, but she never imagined the hobby would lead to a brick-and-mortar shop. Today, her hand-stitched, buttery-soft leather totes and handbags have become staples for locals. Drop by to see the lovingly made offerings, plus a funky selection of jewelry, scarves, and home accessories from fellow female designers.

» **Don't leave without** perusing the eclectic collection of secondhand items sourced from around the world, such as antique Chinese stools.

ORE BY SOPHIE HUGHES
Map 2; 681 Tremont Street, South End; ///worked.wipe.being; www.sophiehughes.com

This appointment-only boutique spotlights the work of indie jewelry makers who use environmentally and socially responsible materials. The store is also carbon-neutral (and is working toward being carbon negative) and is pledging at least 1 percent of its sales to environmental projects. Oh, and did we mention that the jewelry is awesome, too? We love the rough-hewn yet delicate bangles and recycled gold engagement rings.

MARIE GALVIN MILLINERY
Map 2; 450 Harrison Avenue, Suite 1, South End; ///economies.crew.epic; www.mariegalvin.com

Two decades ago, millinery wasn't on Boston's radar (apart from the beloved Red Sox cap, of course). Then Marie Galvin came along, turning the city's fashion scene on its head (pun intended) with her hand-crafted headgear. Inside her boudoir-esque store, you'll find folks trying on headbands, fascinators, and hats worthy of the Kentucky Derby – because who doesn't want a pillbox hat adorned with pink orchids?

SALMAGUNDI

Map 5; 765 Centre Street, Jamaica Plain; ///game.adopt.clever;
www.salmagundiboston.com

Flat caps, cloches, fedoras: when it comes to hats, Salmagundi has got every type imaginable (there's an estimated 10,000 in store). Many of the items that you'll see stacked floor to ceiling are designed by Jessen and Andria, the store's hat-loving owners. They often treat customers to a tour of the collection, offering to jazz up any chosen headgear with ribbons or feather trims. Hats off to them.

MICHELLE MERCALDO

Map 2; 276 Shawmut Avenue, South End; ///taped.woof.pace;
www.michelemercaldojewelry.com

Award-winning designer Michelle Mercaldo believes in the beauty of combining something old with something new. Her stunning, handcrafted pieces often feature recycled metals and stones, which

Shh!

Looking for some sneakers to finish off your look? Head to speakeasy-style Bodega (*www.bdgastore.com*). In what looks like a run-down corner store, a secret door (hidden behind an old vending machine) leads to shelves of cutting-edge sneakers, plus a curated selection of streetwear. Come to browse for big-name brands like Lacoste and Adidas, as well as this offbeat spot's very own in-house line.

are transformed into cool, contemporary offerings with a minimalist edge. She'll even upcycle your old heirlooms, giving them a modern twist; imagine your grandmother's pearl studs remodeled as gold-encased drop earrings.

» Don't leave without seeing Michelle in action. She fashions all her pieces in-house at the huge wooden work table in the back of the store.

HELEN'S LEATHER
Map 1; 110 Charles Street, Beacon Hill; ///tracks.tile.share;
www.helensleather.com

Marked by a big cowboy boot sign out front, this place is a splash of Americana amid the otherwise quaint streets of historic Beacon Hill. For 30 years, the family-owned shop has been keeping locals looking swell with its amazing selection of cowhide tote bags, jean jackets, and (it goes without saying) cowboy boots. Head here to add a dash of Wild West flare to your wardrobe.

FILOMENA DEMARCO JEWELRY
Map 4; 1 Bow Market Way, Somerville; ///curry.dame.drums;
www.filomenademarcojewelry.com

After earning a degree in metalsmithing from MassArt, Ashley Vick started this store, naming it after her great-grandmother (a trailblazing entrepreneur in the 1920s). The chunky, gemstone-dotted necklaces, rings, and bracelets are true statement pieces, but it's the custom works that are the most eye-catching, such as a person's wisdom teeth turned into a stunning necklace.

Gourmet Treats

Picking out a gift for a food-loving friend? Want to impress at your next dinner party? Or just fancy treating yourself? Pop by one of these spots to snap up some tasty tidbits.

URBAN GRAPE

Map 2; 303 Columbus Avenue, South End; ///vibes.urban.custom; www.theurbangrape.shop

This award-winning wine shop does things a little differently. For one thing, it stocks offbeat wines from smaller vineyards, including a sweet selection of vintages by female, BIPOC, and LGBTQ+ producers. For another, it organizes its wines by "body," rather than region or varietal, making it super-easy to pick the best option for your palate. Pop by to grab something unique for your next dinner party.

SEED

Map 5; 401 Centre Street A, Jamaica Plain; ///audit.places.modest; www.seedyourhead.com

Massachusetts was one of the first US states to legalize weed, so it's no surprise that Boston has a great selection of dispensaries stocking all sorts of adult treats. This edgy basement in Jamaica

Plain is one of the best, offering folks from across the city yummy varieties of gummies, chocolates, and other delights. Big faves are the infused ice creams and chocolate cheesecake-flavored candies. **» Don't leave without** visiting the store's Core Social Justice Cannabis Museum, which explores the consequences of the US's cannabis laws, especially their disproportionate impacts on communities of color.

FORMAGGIO KITCHEN
Map 2; 268 Shawmut Avenue, South End; ///riders.spout.farmer; www.formaggiokitchen.com

Formaggio truly has the word on curd. The counter inside this cute store overflows with over 200 cheeses – from rare Comté to bloomy brie to the best nutty Parmesan – all sourced from across Europe. These creamy delights cluster in wheels, hunks, and slivers, all just waiting to be tasted. In fact, the store's super-friendly and knowledge-able staff eagerly encourage customers to find their perfect match, and will offer near endless samples until you find the one (just don't come here before dinner).

Try it!
CHEESY STORAGE

Book a tour of Formaggio's cheese caves, found below their Cambridge store. Accompanied by expert cheesemongers, you'll learn about the nuances of storing cheese and, of course, do some sampling.

Solo, Pair, Crowd

Shopping solo? Out with the gang? Whoever you're with, Boston has plenty of places to grab edible treats.

FLYING SOLO
No buds needed

Come and have a chat with the friendly budtenders at Pure Oasis. They really know their stuff: this Black-owned, community-focused store was Boston's first recreational cannabis dispensary.

IN A PAIR
Furry friends

After an energetic run around Peters Park in the South End, take your best (canine) pal to nearby Polka Dog Bakery. This specialty pet shop makes its own delicious gourmet dog biscuits.

FOR A CROWD
Market munchies

The city's OG food hall, Boston Public Market has local grub to satisfy every member of your squad, whether they have a craving for super-fresh smoothies or smoked fish.

EHCHOCOLATIER

Map 6; 145 Huron Avenue, Cambridge; ///picked.worked.dwell;
www.ehchocolatier.com

Friends Elaine and Catherine set up shop over two decades ago and
have been churning out scrumptious handmade sweets ever since.
Whatever chocolatey confection you have affection for – bonbons,
chocolate bars, truffles – you'll find it in this tiny chocolatier.
» Don't leave without a Boston icon chocolate box, which contains
chocs decorated with sketches of city landmarks.

CURIO SPICE CO.

Map 4; 2265 Massachusetts Avenue, Cambridge; ///upset.dame.blows;
www.curiospice.com

Jars, vials, and amber glass bottles line the shelves at Curio, each filled
with delicious spices sourced from owner Clare's travels across Asia
and beyond. Clare makes sure everything is procured directly from
the producers themselves, meaning fresher spices, a smaller carbon
footprint, and more money to the farmers that deserve it.

ARAX MARKET

Map 6; 585 Mount Auburn Street, Watertown; ///parents.gangs.catch;
617-924-3399

Long-standing regulars drop by this mom-and-pop Armenian market,
run by the same family since 1974, to stock up on Mediterranean
and Middle Eastern staples. Think baba ganoush, pita bread, and
falafel, plus delicious housemade pistachio baklava and rose jam.

CHARLES STREET

REVERE STREET

Pop into
RUGG ROAD PAPER COMPANY

This eclectic stationery store celebrates the lost art of letter-writing. Here you'll find handmade paper, greeting cards, and ribbons galore.

Refuel at
BLANK STREET COFFEE

Pause at this tiny coffee cart. Part of a mini-chain founded by two friends, it serves up aromatic coffee and freshly made pastries.

Louisburg Square *was once home to both the American novelist Louisa May Alcott and the former Secretary of State John Kerry.*

PINCKNEY STREET

Shop preloved at
FABLED ANTIQUES

Unearth varied antique and vintage items, from American Impressionist paintings to Victorian cake pedestals.

WEST CEDAR STREET

BEACON HILL

Louisburg Square

CHARLES STREET

Lose track of time in
BEACON HILL BOOKS & CAFE

Housed in a glorious old townhouse, this five-story bookstore feels super homey, thanks to its painted shelves and comfy chairs.

MOUNT VERNON STREE

ACORN STREET

Begin with a browse at
DECEMBER THIEVES

Packed with fashion-forward threads, hand-stitched bags, and more, this women-owned store champions small-batch artists and designers.

Thanks to its charming cobblestones and vintage gas lamps, pretty **Acorn Street** *is one of the most photographed locations in all of Boston.*

CHESTNUT STREET

CHARLES STREET

REVERE   STREET

MYRTLE   STREET

PINCKNEY   STREET

CHESTNUT   STREET

A morning shopping on
Charles Street

Sure, upscale Newbury Street might be Boston's famous shopping hub, but insiders know that Charles Street is actually the best spot in the city if you're looking for boutique buys. Tracing a line through Boston's leafy Beacon Hill neighborhood – famous for its cobblestone streets and historic red-brick brownstones – this charming avenue is home to a community of cool indie stores. Head here to browse for stylish threads, locally made jewelry, and offbeat vintage finds.

1. December Thieves
51 Charles Street, Beacon Hill; www.decemberthieves.com
///pinks.older.super

2. Beacon Hill Books & Cafe
71 Charles Street, Beacon Hill; www.bhbooks.com
///fees.define.flap

3. Fabled Antiques
93 Charles Street, Beacon Hill; 617-936-3008
///silent.ranks.media

4. Blank Street Coffee
97 Charles Street , Beacon Hill; www.blankstreet.com
///liability.fluid.crib

5. Rugg Road Paper Company
105 Charles Street, Beacon Hill; www.ruggroadpaper.com
///mash.fuel.acute

Acorn Street
///class.glitz.green

Louisburg Square
///next.salt.crest

ARTS & CULTURE

Mixing historic sights and literary haunts with innovative museums and free-thinking street art, Boston's cultural scene is an exciting blend of the old and the new.

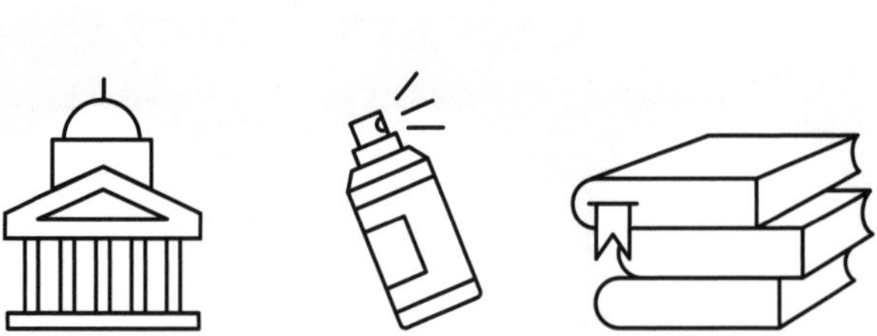

City History

From the American Revolution and abolitionism to the fight for LGBTQ+ rights and beyond, Boston has been at the forefront of many history-changing movements and moments.

BOSTON IRISH FAMINE MEMORIAL

Map 1; corner of Washington and School streets, Downtown; ///builds.dime.teach

Between 1845 and 1849, around 100,000 Irish refugees arrived in Boston, fleeing Ireland's potato famine, otherwise known as the "Great Hunger." This poignant memorial, a collection of eight life-size bronze sculptures, depicts the difficulties experienced by these early immigrants and how they went on to thrive in their new home.

BLACK HERITAGE TRAIL

Map 1; Massachusetts 54th Regiment Memorial, Beacon Hill; ///kept.after.skills; www.nps.gov/boaf

Beacon Hill was a crucible of action against slavery in the 1800s. Home to a tight-knit community of free African Americans, the area was an important stop-off on the Underground Railroad and an instrumental player in the Abolition Movement. Explore its history on the 1.6-mile (2.5-km) Black Heritage Trail, which winds past sights like the home of Lewis and Harriet Hayden, a key safehouse on the railroad. The trail ends at the Museum of African American History, a fascinating spot that includes both the 1806 African Meeting House, where abolitionist Frederick Douglass spoke, and the Abiel Smith School, the country's first school for Black students. **» Don't leave without** also walking the Women's Suffrage Trail, which takes in key sights linked to women's fight for the right to vote.

OLD SOUTH MEETING HOUSE

Map 1; 310 Washington Street, Downtown; ///guess.grape.bumpy;
www.revolutionaryspaces.org/old-south-meeting-house

During the 18th century, "Old South" was a regular hub for protest meetings against British control of the US. On December 16, 1793, some 5,000 people fervently discussed the idea of "no taxation without representation." The meeting whipped up public feeling and, later that evening, led to what is now known as the Boston Tea Party – an event that helped ignite the American Revolution.

Try it!
TAKE THE FREEDOM TRAIL

"Old South" is an early stop on Boston's Freedom Trail (www.thefreedomtrail.org). Connecting 16 historic sights, including many linked to the Revolution, this 2.5-mile (4-km) walking tour delves into Boston's rich past.

KING'S CHAPEL BURYING GROUND

Map 1; 58 Tremont Street, Downtown; ///plot.entire.insist

Established in the 17th century, this tiny patch of green is the oldest cemetery in Boston. Seek out the grave of Mary Chilton, the very first woman to step off the *Mayflower*, then wander over to the resting place of Thomas Brattle, one of the first people to speak out against the Salem Witch Trials. The most visited grave, though, is that of a little-known shop owner named Joseph Tapping. His carved headstone depicts a battle between Death and Father Time.

CAMBRIDGE CITY HALL

Map 4; 795 Massachusetts Avenue, Cambridge; ///cost.thus.pines

This chateau-like building was the setting of a landmark event back in 2004. Just after the clock struck midnight on May 17, it became the first place in the US to start issuing same-sex marriage licenses.

Shh!

Just off Battery Street in the North End is All Saints Way, a striking shrine dedicated to Catholic saints. The collection, which includes photos, statues, and prayer cards, is the handiwork of Peter Baldassari, a neighborhood local who has been collecting saint-related memorabilia since he was a kid. Over the years, visitors from all over the world have come to glimpse the shrine, adding their own items to the holy display. If you're very lucky, Peter might even offer you a tour.

A huge party was held for the 260 couples who registered, complete with a three-tiered wedding cake and live music. Hours later, the hall hosted another inaugural event: the first same-sex wedding in the US.

DEER ISLAND NIPMUC MEMORIAL

Map 6; Deer Island, Winthrop; ///rumbles.beanstalk.smothered

This sobering plaque commemorates a bleak event that took place in the mid-17th century. Driven by an irrational fear of attack, New England colonists imprisoned the area's Indigenous Nipmuc people on Deer Island, a tiny atoll in Boston Harbor, leading to the deaths of hundreds of men, women, and children from disease and starvation. Every October, their descendants hold a ceremony at the memorial, honoring the memory of those who tragically lost their lives here.

» **Don't leave without** planning a trip to the Pilgrim Monument and Provincetown Museum on Cape Cod *(p181)*, which has an exhibit on the area's Indigenous communities, told from their own perspective.

FENWAY PARK LIVING MUSEUM

Map 3; 4 Yawkey Way, Fenway; ///kind.trash.drag;
www.mlb.com/redsox/ballpark/museum

Bostonians are so proud of their legendary baseball team, the Red Sox, that they opened a museum in their honor. Housed inside Fenway Park, the team's home, this shrine to the Sox contains more than 170,000 pieces of memorabilia dating back to the 1930s, including uniforms and bats from legends like Ted Williams and Babe Ruth. Want to take a peek? Sign up for a tour of the famed ballpark.

Art Galleries

Boston might be better known for sports and science, but its arts scene is just as legendary. Like your art contemporary? More of a purist? Boston has something for every taste.

MASSART MUSEUM

Map 3; 621 Huntington Avenue, Mission Hill; ///form.soccer.memory; www.massart.edu/galleries/massart-art-museum

After a class, this campus museum is usually jam-packed with students looking for creative inspo. Luckily for them, there's a near-constant supply here, thanks to the ever-changing roster of thought-provoking exhibitions. Past shows have included multimedia works paying homage to inspiring women and pieces criticizing the American patriarchy.

MUSEUM OF FINE ARTS

Map 3; 465 Huntington Avenue, Fenway; ///affair.turned.cargo; www.mfa.org

Say hello to the grand dame of Boston's art museums. Inside the Beaux Arts building, awestruck out-of-towners and locals alike come together to admire the world-class collection of fine art.

Watch out for the Late Nite events, which see DJs, dancing, and more take over the MFA.

Check out pieces from heavyweights like Claude Monet and Frida Kahlo, but don't sleep on the museum's selection of Korean art – it's one of the largest in the world.

INSTITUTE OF CONTEMPORARY ART
Map 5; 24 Harbor Shore Drive, Seaport; ///goals.stray.dash;
www.icaboston.org

You'll find a cool crowd hanging at this harborside museum, which is packed with cutting-edge contemporary art. Past exhibitions have included Yayoi Kusama's trippy mirrored rooms and a collection celebrating late fashion icon Virgil Abloh. Many solo careers have been launched here (think Kai Althoff and Nan Goldin) so you might just spot a new rising star in the art world.

» Don't leave without visiting the ICA's Watershed, a venue for rotating immersive exhibits found just across the Boston Harbor.

ISABELLA STEWART GARDNER MUSEUM
Map 3; 25 Evans Way, Fenway; ///employ.petal.cats;
www.gardnermuseum.org

The eponymous Isabella is as much of an icon now as she was during the late 19th century. An eccentric socialite, she traveled through Europe, the Middle East, Asia, and beyond, amassing an eclectic art collection of Japanese scroll paintings, Iranian ceramics, and much more besides. Leave enough time to linger in the Venetian-style interior courtyard, where stunning floral displays change seasonally.

Solo, Pair, Crowd

Ponder a piece of art in peace or discuss with your gang – whatever you like to do, Boston has a gallery for it.

FLYING SOLO
Studio exploring
On Sunday afternoons, the artists at SoWa open their studios to the public. Come to admire their work and have a chat with other art lovers – or even the artists themselves, if they're around.

IN A PAIR
Cyber sessions
Take a tech-minded friend to the Boston Cyberarts Gallery. Found in a rail station, this avant-garde joint focuses on electronic and digital art, including pieces made using augmented reality.

FOR A CROWD
Three's the magic number
The Harvard Art Museums are comprised of three separate galleries under one roof. Explore them with a gang of friends at one of the evening lates; grab a drink, listen to live music, and take a tour of the galleries.

MUSEUM OF BAD ART

Map 5; 1250 Massachusetts Avenue, Dorchester; ///silks.press.luck; www.museumofbadart.org

They say art is subjective, but the stuff you'll find here is, well, bad. Curated from estate sales, dumpsters, and the like, the works range from the silly to the strange. A dog juggling bones? Check. Medusa frying a fish? You got it. A woman riding a lobster? You know the score.

NATIONAL CENTER OF AFRO-AMERICAN ARTISTS

Map 5; 300 Walnut Street, Roxbury; ///deals.driven.shave; www.ncaaa.org

Housed in a gorgeous brownstone, this spot celebrates the work of Black artists from Boston and beyond. Don't miss the large-scale head sculpture out front; it was made by local artist John Wilson, whose work explores themes of racial justice.

DORCHESTER ART PROJECT

Map 5; 1490 Dorchester Avenue, Dorchester; ///dozen.damp.clever; www.dorchesterartproject.com

As well as studio and performance spaces, this cool community joint hosts exhibitions featuring pieces made by local artists. Much of the work has an experimental vibe, with previous shows focusing on topics like mental health and queer perspectives.

» **Don't leave without** checking out the project's events calendar, which features amazing live music shows and open-mic nights.

Favorite Museums

*Science, sport, subcultures – whatever you want
to learn about, there's a museum for it in Boston.
Even better, some have late-night openings and
a whole bunch of awesome events.*

BOSTON MUSEUM OF SCIENCE

**Map 1; 1 Museum of Science Driveway, West End; ///meals.icons.voted;
www.mos.org**

This institution's dinosaurs, dioramas, and live presentations are
iconic. During the day, tourists and school groups rule the roost, but
come nightfall, the museum is the domain of adults-only. Then,
9-to-5ers arrive for the museum's SubSpace events, which might
cover talks on the patriarchy, movie screenings celebrating women

Try it!
SEE THE STARS

Boston University's Coit Observatory *(www.
bu.edu)* has public astronomy sessions every
Wednesday after sundown. An expert will
point out the stars and planets, and answer
burning questions. Buy tickets in advance.

explorers, or sound bath sessions. Some of the best offerings take place in the planetarium: one evening you can pop by for a Led Zeppelin laser show, the next a drag performance.

JOHN F. KENNEDY PRESIDENTIAL LIBRARY AND MUSEUM

Map 5; Columbia Point, Dorchester; ///fills.bars.festivity; www.jfklibrary.org

This coastal complex is a window into the life and times of the Kennedy dynasty, especially its most famous son: Boston-born John F. Kennedy. Items include his World War II tags and 25-ft- (7.6-m-) long sailboat, as well as designer gowns worn by First Lady Jackie. Signing up for a tour is recommended.

THE MAPPARIUM

Map 3; 210 Massachusetts Avenue, Back Bay; ///wing.stack.gather; www.marybakereddylibrary.org

Hidden away in the Mary Baker Eddy Library, this inside-out globe is a sight to behold: no surprise, really, since it stands three stories high and is made entirely of stained glass. Stroll along through the sphere's center to see the world's borders as they were in 1935, when the globe was made. You'll also discover the real size and position of each continent – without any distortion from perspective or politics. Spoiler alert: Europe is tiny.

» Don't leave without playing around with the acoustics – the curved walls of the Mapparium act as a "whispering gallery."

Liked by the locals

"The passion of Boston sports fans runs deep. They've cheered on the likes of the Red Sox and Bruins for decades, supporting their teams through thick and thin, ups and downs. That is the true test of devotion."

BRIAN CODAGNONE, ASSOCIATE CURATOR
AT THE SPORTS MUSEUM

THE SPORTS MUSEUM
Map 1; TD Garden, 100 Legends Way, West End;
///kicked.ladder.deflection; www.sportsmuseum.org

Sport is sacred in Boston, and this is where the faithful come to worship. The history of teams like the Sox and Celtics is recounted in full glory, with relics (including basketball legend Shaquille O'Neal's sneakers) on display. To enter, join a tour of TD Garden (p177).

MIT MUSEUM
Map 4; Gambrill Center, 314 Main Street, Cambridge;
///monks.rush.awake; https://mitmuseum.mit.edu

The innovative exhibits at MIT's in-house museum are a must-see, but have you heard about the adults-only After Dark sessions? Accompanied by live music, these interactive events explore things like the chemistry of cocktails and the science behind magnetic attractions.

» Don't leave without checking out the museum's other events, including science-focused discussions and documentary screenings.

GIBSON HOUSE MUSEUM
Map 2; 137 Beacon Street, Back Bay; ///skills.state.moons;
www.thegibsonhouse.org

This charming brownstone provides a snapshot of life in the 18th and 19th centuries. Among its previous owners was Charlie Gibson, Jr., a member of the city's once-hidden gay community. If you're there on the first Thursday of the month, join one of the tours that focuses on Boston's gay subculture around the 1900s – a tribute to Charlie.

Literary Locations

Louisa May Alcott, Ralph Waldo Emerson, Edgar Allan Poe – these literary greats have all called Boston home. Bookish haunts hark back to their glory days, while historic libraries lure in new readers.

PINCKNEY STREET

Map 1; Pinckney Street, Beacon Hill; ///swung.grant.curry

Cobbled sidewalks, old-school street lamps, and brick row houses: Pinckney Street is charm itself. And we're not the only ones who think so. Numerous writers have put down roots here: philosopher Henry David Thoreau lived at number 4, Irish poet Louise Imogen Guiney at number 16, and Louisa May Alcott (of *Little Women* fame) at numbers 20, 43, and 81. Just imagine the kind of neighborhood book club they would have enjoyed had they crossed paths...

EDGAR ALLAN POE STATUE

Map 2; Edgar Allan Poe Square, Back Bay; ///about.woof.worked

The dark poet – aka Edgar Allan Poe – was born in Boston's Back Bay in 1809. Though Poe died in 1849, he's been forever immortalized through this statue, which shows him striding forward, cloak billowing behind and a trail of papers spilling out of his briefcase. Fans of the

The square is the gateway to Boston's literary district – check out the map at *www.boston litdistrict.org/map*.

macabre will love the nods to some of his most famous morbid works, from the raven flying ahead of him to the heart emerging from his case.

THE PRINTING OFFICE OF EDES & GILL

Map 1; 21 Unity Street, North End; ///cherry.spray.state;
www.bostongazette.com

This tiny spot is a reproduction of the print shop that once published the *Boston Gazette*, one of the most politically radical pre-Revolution newspapers. Owner Gary Gregory is a total legend: he'll expound on the history of printing and give demos of how to use the press – all while dressed head-to-toe in colonial garb.

» Don't leave without picking up a freshly printed copy of the world-famous Declaration of Independence.

GRAVE OF E. E. CUMMINGS

Map 5; Forest Hills Cemetery, 95 Forest Hills Avenue, Jamaica Plain;
///detect.looked.swing; www.foresthillscemetary.com

For lit lovers, a stroll through leafy Forest Hills Cemetery wouldn't be complete without a visit to one of its most famous residents: iconic poet E. E. Cummings. Pay your respects at the humble plaque sitting on the grass (it's found just to the right of his wife's "Clarke" family stone), then keep wandering. You'll stumble upon the resting spots of many other notable writers, including 19th-century cookbook author Fannie Farmer and Noble Prize-winning playwright Eugene O'Neill.

BOSTON PUBLIC LIBRARY
CENTRAL BRANCH

Map 2; 700 Boylston Street, Back Bay; ///heap.tape.humble; www.bpl.org

The main branch of the BPL is always buzzing: students study, academics peruse the stacks, and wide-eyed tourists admire the building's gorgeous decor, complete with giant ceiling frescoes. Make for the Bates Reading Room, where the classic library vibes (think polished wood tables topped with bankers lamps) will inspire you to write your magnum opus. Want to kick back with a book? Perch up in the serene Italian-style central courtyard.

OMNI PARKER HOUSE

Map 1; 60 School Street, Downtown; ///shot.undulation.crown; www.omnihotels.com/hotels/boston-parker-house

If the walls of this historic hotel could talk, they'd share stories of the exclusive "Saturday Club" that met here in the mid-1800s. The group would discuss books, politics, and philosophy, cigars in hand; among

Try it!
PUT PEN TO PAPER

Looking to polish your writing skills?
Book onto a creative writing workshop
at Grub Street (www.grubstreet.org).
This center offers a wide range of tutorials
on things like novel- and playwriting.

them were literary greats such as Henry Wadsworth Longfellow. The bookish ties don't stop there, though: Charles Dickens once performed a reading of *A Christmas Carol* in the restaurant, while Edith Wharton has spent the night here. The hotel even features in her celebrated novel, *The Age of Innocence*.

» Don't leave without trying a slice of the famous Boston cream pie (a cream-filled sponge cake) at the restaurant, its original birthplace.

RUINS OF SCHOOLMASTER HILL
Map 5; Franklin Park, 1 Franklin Park Road, Roxbury;
///lion.grape.models

Found in leafy Franklin Park *(p167)*, this small rise was once home to writer and philosopher Ralph Waldo Emerson. He lived in a cabin here for two years while working as a schoolmaster (hence the hill's name). Though the house itself is gone, you can still wander through the ruins and soak up the natural beauty that inspired his work.

BOSTON ATHENAEUM
Map 1; 10½ Beacon Street, Beacon Hill; ///alarm.drips.august;
www.bostonathenaeum.org

Dating back to 1807, this members-only library is home to over half a million books, artworks, and artifacts, including a collection of items from the American Civil War. Inside, it's all old-world vibes: austere marble busts gaze down at well-read locals, who come to peruse the tome-packed stacks or hunker down on one of the elegant patterned sofas. To enter, grab a day pass or join one of the weekly guided tours.

Public Art

Boston is awash with outdoor art, with many of the pieces having a strong political or community focus. New projects are regularly in the works, but these pieces are some of the city's best and most beloved.

THE EMBRACE

Map 1; 139 Tremont Street, Boston Common; ///gangs.blows.noses

This gleaming, 22-ft- (7-m-) high brass sculpture honors civil rights activists Dr. Martin Luther King, Jr. and Coretta Scott King, who met in Boston in the 1950s while studying. An intertwining of four arms, the piece was inspired by a 1964 photo of the two Kings embracing after learning Martin Luther had won the Nobel Peace Prize. Fittingly, it lives on Boston Common, the site of many public rallies and peaceful protests – including one led by Dr. King himself in 1965.

RITA'S SPOTLIGHT

Map 6; 506 Cambridge Street, Allston; ///spine.over.pure

Painted by local artist Rixy, this colorful mural commemorates Rita Hester, a Black trans woman and beloved member of the Allston community who died as a result of transphobic violence. Though few know her name, her murder in 1998 led to the creation of the

Transgender Day of Remembrance, which, on November 20th every year, honors those trans lives lost to homicide. The powerful piece shows Rita surrounded by the colors of the trans pride flag, as well as her favorite cheetah print and an excerpt from one of her poems.

ALCHEMIST
Map 4; Stratton Student Center Lawn, Massachusetts Avenue, Kendall Square; ///watch.heavy.mess

Created by Spanish artist Jaume Plensa, this stainless steel sculpture is an homage to MIT's scientists and researchers. Made up of a mix of numbers and mathematical symbols, it depicts a seated figure with their knees drawn into their chest, as if in quiet contemplation. Walk inside the sculpture to get a new angle on the piece – after all, the best ideas come from looking at things from a new perspective, right?

DON'T LET ME BE MISUNDERSTOOD
Map 2; 90 Traveler Street, South End; ///ample.regime.estate

Head to Underground at Ink Block (a highway underpass repurposed as an urban park) to take in this powerful piece. The work of Rob Gibbs and Victor Quiñonez (aka ProBlak and Marka27), this mural provokes a dialogue about racial inequities both past and present. A raised fist for solidarity stands at the center, surrounded by two portraits of singer and civil rights activist Nina Simone (one of whose songs inspired the work's name), plus figures representing injustice and hope.

» Don't leave without viewing *No Weapon Formed Against Thee Shall Prosper*, also located in the park, which honors victims of police brutality.

DEATH TO PLASTIC

Map 6; 160 Liverpool Street, East Boston; ///shirts.potato.pumps

This bright, comic book-style mural gets to the heart of one of the big environmental issues of our time: plastic pollution. Made by Tallboy, a local illustrator and tattoo artist, the piece depicts a skull-filled plastic bottle encircled by a giant octopus. The bottle remains intact – much like billions of plastic products found all over our planet today. It's a positive reminder to keep ditching all that single-use plastic.

MAKE WAY FOR DUCKLINGS

Map 1; Boston Public Garden, Back Bay; ///improving.cabin.candle

Made by artist Nancy Schön, these little bronze ducklings are totally adorable. The sculptures are based on Robert McCloskey's beloved kids' book about a family of ducks who make their way to a new home in Boston Public Garden. Depending on the time of year,

Shh!

As you stroll around Boston, you might spy colorful electric utility boxes dotted here and there. These normally practical structures have been painted with flowers, geometric shapes, jellyfish, cityscapes, and more. Why? Well, it's all thanks to the City of Boston's PaintBox project, which commissions local artists to embellish the city-owned utility boxes. The cheerful pops of color add some much-appreciated pizzazz to these otherwise gray and boring metal blocks.

these fluffy fellas might be dressed up in Easter bonnets or little winter scarves. And being Bostonians, they're big sports fans, too, so don't be surprised if they don team colors anytime a local team is in the play-offs.

WE ARE ALL STREAMS LEADING TO THE SAME RIVER

Map 3; 104 Forsyth Street, Northeastern University; ///bats.miles.star
Wrapping around three sides of Northeastern University's Latinx Student Cultural Center, this kaleidoscopic mural is a celebration of Latin American cultures. It was created by renowned San Francisco muralist Susan Kelk Cervantes and the artists of Precita Eyes (one of the few community mural arts centers in the US), with help from students and university staff. Check out the nods to different communities, including a colorful ribbon of flags from the Americas.
» Don't leave without checking out the other art on Northeastern's campus, including 3D sculptures, rotating exhibits, and more murals.

SANGRE INDIGENA

Map 3; 75 Malcolm X Boulevard, Roxbury; ///stick.noting.broke
This eye-catching mural was created by Don Rimx to draw attention to the continued MMIW (missing and murdered Indigenous women) crisis that affects America, Canada, and Latin America. The powerful piece depicts an Indigenous woman with a red handprint over her lower face, and has been painted using bright colors separated by chunky black lines, giving it an almost stained-glass look.

STREET

WASHINGTON STREET

TRAVELER STREET

HARRISON AVENUE

Grab a bite at
FUJI AT INK BLOC

End your morning by
snacking on artfully
arranged plates of sush
and sashimi at this slee
Japanese joint.

TRAVELER STREET

EAST

BERKELEY

STREET

Peters
Park

WASHINGTON STREET

Discover new talents at
MASS ART X SOWA

Showcasing works by students
and graduates of MassArt,
this gallery is the place to pick
up something by the next big
name in the Boston art scene.

SOUTH
END

ALBANY STREET

HARRISON AVENUE

THAYER

STREET

Grab a flat white at
MOD ESPRESSO

This stylish coffee bar is
attached to sleek design store
Modern Relik, which sells
contemporary artworks and
stunning art and design books.

SoWa Art District's
First Friday *event
(first Friday of every
month) sees artists open
their studio doors to
the public.*

JOHN F. FITZGERALD EXPRESSW

JOHN F. FITZGERALD EXPRESSW

An arty morning in
SoWa

Look up at
UNDERGROUND
AT INK BLOCK
Take a stroll through this
highway underpass and
admire the colorful murals
splashed across its walls
and columns.

3

JOHN F. FITZGERALD EXPRESSWAY

There's no denying it, Boston's art scene is thriving.
The city's home to way more than its fair share of
world-famous art museums, indie galleries, and,
of course, MassArt (Massachusetts College of
Art and Design). A particular hot spot for artistic
activity is SoWa, the area south of Washington
Street in the South End. This once-forgotten
industrial area is now a dedicated art and design
district, where abandoned warehouses host
working studios and cutting-edge galleries.

1. Mod Espresso
485 Harrison Avenue;
www.mod-espresso.com
///wallet.owls.books

2. MassArt x SoWa
460 Harrison Avenue;
www.sowa.massart.edu
///grace.entire.rear

**3. Underground at
Ink Block**
90 Traveler Street; www.
undergroundinkblock.com
///grace.entire.rear

4. Fuji at Ink Block
352b Harrison Avenue;
www.fujiatinkblock.com
///yappy.jumps.tall

First Friday
///achieving.worth.life

NIGHTLIFE

Nights out in Boston are pretty easygoing. Stand-up acts keep the laughs coming, musicians jam in intimate venues, and avant-garde plays provide plenty to mull over.

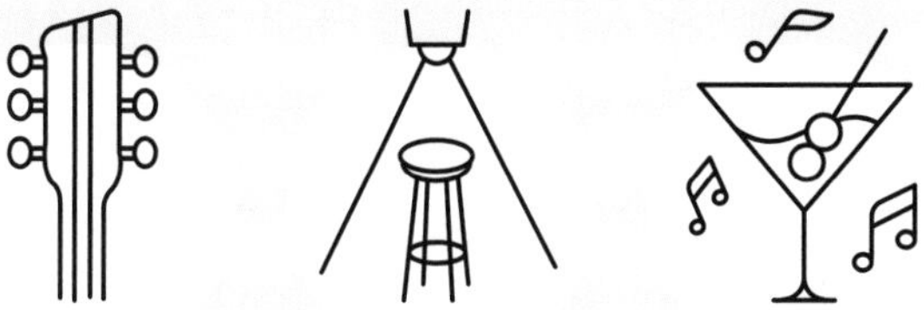

Music Venues

Live music is the heartbeat of Boston's nightlife scene. The city is home to more than its fair share of amazing venues, from big concert halls to low-key joints. Just remember to buy your tickets ahead of time.

CLUB PASSIM

Map 4; 47 Palmer Street, Cambridge; ///privately.vouch.head; www.passim.org

Just west of Harvard Yard, this cozy basement venue is best known for launching the careers of folk greats like Bob Dylan and Joan Baez. For such a famous spot, the space is unpretentiously simple: one small, nondescript room packed with close-knit tables. The intimate shows here are the haunt of the usual eclectic Cambridge crowd (students, academics, artists), who drop in for great music and chill vibes.

WALLY'S CAFE JAZZ CLUB

Map 3; 427 Massachusetts Avenue, Roxbury; ///rocket.skinny.shops; www.wallyscafe.com

A testament to Roxbury's historic affinity for jazz, this joint has been popping off with live music since 1947. It was set up by Barbadian immigrant Joseph L. Walcott (aka "Wally"), who opened the club with the savings he had from working odd jobs, becoming New England's first Black nightclub owner in the process. Today, a mix of Roxbury regulars and students from Boston's many music schools pack into the old-school space for funky nights of impromptu jazz.

ROADRUNNER

Map 6; 89 Guest Street, Brighton; ///trains.nights.wisdom; www.roadrunnerboston.com

One of Boston's larger music venues, this no-frills place plays host to big-name bands, including the likes of indie icons The National and Modest Mouse. But size isn't everything: the venue also has killer acoustics, state-of-the-art equipment, and four big bars to keep you fueled as you bop across the floor. And while indie rock is big here, pop-punk, folk, dubstep, and more all make an appearance.

CAFE 939

Map 3; 939 Boylston Street, Back Bay; ///many.bunch.trials; www.berklee.edu/cafe939

Catch the next big thing at tiny Cafe 939, a super-chill, clubby spot doused in red lighting. It's run by students from Berklee College of Music, who show off their skills at the recurring open-mic nights (don't be surprised if their professors start a jam session, either). Alongside the local talent, there's also an eclectic selection of touring artists, ranging from disco-funk groups to soulful singer-songwriter acts.

» Don't leave without popping by the more buttoned-up Berklee Performance Center, the college's in-house venue, across the street.

LIZARD LOUNGE

Map 4; 1667 Massachusetts Avenue, Cambridge; ///added.care.passes;
www.lizardloungeclub.com

Inside this moody basement club, you'll be greeted with an energy akin to the grimy (but great) venues that your friend's high-school band played at. Join the music school students and bona fide hippies who flock to the cavelike interior nightly, where everyone from rock bands to hip-hop acts to Bavarian folk groups grace the stage.

» Don't leave without making a plan to come back with the gang on Sunday night, when the lounge hosts one of its popular poetry jams.

BRIGHTON MUSIC HALL

Map 6; 158 Brighton Avenue, Allston; ///shins.spray.begun;
www.crossroadspresents.com/pages/brighton-music-hall-inner

Any local who went through a punk or emo phase spent many nights of their youth yelling their lungs out here. Today, the lineup has a great selection of genres, from roots-rock bands like The Blasters to the industrial goth artist Ohgr. Hang out in the back by the pool tables or get close enough to the stage to high-five the band.

PARADISE ROCK CLUB

Map 3; 967 Commonwealth Avenue, Allston; ///crash.theme.settle;
www.crossroadspresents.com/pages/paradise-rock-club

After rock 'n' roll vibes? Head to Paradise Rock Club. Housed in an old industrial space, this club has been an iconic part of the city's music scene since it first opened in the 1970s. Some of the biggest

Arrive early to grab a drink at the bar before it gets busy – and to get a place in front of the stage.

and best rock bands in the biz have played here, including U2, Kings of Leon, and AC/DC, but there's often a fair few up-and-coming local acts, too.

SCULLERS JAZZ CLUB

Map 4; 400 Soldiers Field Road, Allston; ///loser.hung.newly; www.scullersjazz.com

Don't be fooled by the modest space or the hotel-chain location; this 200-seat joint is one of Boston's most prestigious jazz venues. As well as hosting jazz icons and Grammy award winners, such as Chick Corea and Nicholas Payton, the club makes an effort to showcase young musicians from local universities. You might even catch a set from a soon-to-be jazz legend as you nestle down in the super-chill, candlelit lounge.

LILYPAD

Map 4; 1353 Cambridge Street, Cambridge; ///chins.loyal.sulk; www.lilypadinman.com

Run by jazz pianist Gill Aharon, super-tiny Lilypad started off as a DIY music venue where locals would come to casually jam. Today, the award-winning space hosts a range of avant-garde performances from classical musicians, indie rockers, and, of course, jazz acts (Gill's own band plays here weekly). It's not just music at this community-focused spot either; other events include storytelling sessions, art shows, and yoga classes.

Comedy Nights

Orange Line delayed again? Sox lost their last game? No worries – Boston's comedy clubs will put a smile back on your face. Whether it's saucy skits or offbeat improv, belly laughs are guaranteed.

IMPROVBOSTON

Map 4; 620 Massachusetts Avenue, Cambridge; ///potato.notice.wallet; www.improvboston.com

This troupe has been getting big laughs out of Bostonians for nearly four decades. Many comics who honed their jokes here have hit the big time, with alumni going on to work on shows like *Drunk History*. Drop in for the signature monthly show for spur-of-the-moment fun and some hilarious audience participation.

Try it!
COMEDY CLASSES

In need of a little improv practice before you make your big debut? ImprovBoston offers lots of workshops for eager comics, with options ranging from a one-time class to intensive courses spanning several months.

THE ROCKWELL

Map 4; 255 Elm Street, Somerville; ///deep.trades.rarely

These basement digs are home to one of the most creative comedy lineups in the city, with the innuendo-packed themed skits a highlight. Join chill Somervillians giggling at Shit-faced Shakespeare (where one of the actors in the play is, erm, a *little* tipsy) or pop by for Dirty Disney (you'll never look at your fave characters the same way).

LAUGH BOSTON

Map 5; 425 Summer Street, Seaport; ///moon.curry.effort; www.laughboston.com

Don't be thrown off by its location inside a business hotel — things get rowdy at Laugh Boston. It's a prime place to catch national acts on tour, but don't just roll through for the big names; this industrial spot also hosts local comics and laugh-out-loud live podcast shows.

» Don't leave without grabbing a quirky cocktail at the bar. Our pick? Go Fish, made with vodka, lemon-lime soda, and Swedish Fish candy.

NICK'S COMEDY STOP

Map 2; 10 Warrenton Street, Bay Village; ///quiet.mason.cafe; www.nickscomedystop.com

Crowds have been packing into Nick's since the 1970s. This no-frills joint is known for its top-notch local talent, who get the crowd chuckling with personal anecdotes and complaints about uniquely Boston problems (oh hi, Orange Line). No probs if you're from out of town — there's no better way to get a handle on local life than catching a show here.

Liked by the locals

"Boston is, somewhat ironically, serious about comedy. Comics will perform at any venue, so long as there's a microphone, and they'll show up an hour early to gigs to work on their material. It's no wonder so many professional comics hail from Boston."

HAL GRIFFIN, COMEDY SHOW HOST AND WRITER

BOSTON COMEDY CLUB

Map 6; 458 Western Avenue, Brighton; ///photo.dining.areas;
www.boscomedyclub.com

This roving comedy club hops between different speakeasy basements come the weekend. A regular haunt is The Hideaway, a hidden tiki bar found under a restaurant. Expect a young, cool, and creative crowd enjoying local acts and big names alike, including folks who have appeared on Comedy Central and *SNL*.

IMPROV ASYLUM

Map 1; 216 Hanover Street, North End; ///counts.them.vets;
www.improvasylum.com

Drop by this North End spot any night of the week for some interactive improv, where audience members are asked to shout out topics to the talented comics on stage. Don't mind the crude and crass? Go for the risqué, yet totally hilarious, midnight "Raunch" shows.

THE COMEDY STUDIO

Map 4; 255 Elm Street, Somerville; ///deep.trades.rarely;
www.thecomedystudio.com

Setting up shop at roving locations, including The Rockwell *(p145)*, this under-the-radar comedy club is consistently packed with Bostonians looking for a good laugh. On stage, expect a thigh-slapping mix of Boston-based budding talent and grizzled comedy veterans.

» Don't leave without grabbing a post-show drink in Spoke Wine Bar, found just down the street from The Rockwell.

LGBTQ+ Scene

Despite the closure of some of Boston's long-standing LGBTQ+ bars and clubs in recent years, the city is still home to a number of cool, queer-friendly spots. These are some of the best.

CLUB CAFÉ

Map 2; 209 Columbus Avenue, Back Bay; ///flash.fault.formal;
www.clubcafe.com

Club Café: modest bistro by day, stalwart of the queer party scene by night. Once the clock strikes 10pm, DJs take center stage, spinning tunes for a packed crowd who bust their best moves beneath a massive disco ball. Not a dancer? No prob – there are queer-friendly events like trivia nights on the regular.

TROPHY ROOM

Map 2; 26 Chandler Street, South End; ///river.burn.dream;
www.trophyroomboston.com

What Trophy Room lacks in size, it makes up for in quirky style; here, funky lime-green furniture contrasts spectacularly with a black-and-white marble floor. Though it's not a gay bar per se, it's become a top pregame spot for queer Bostonians before they head over to nearby

Need to refuel after your night out? Trophy Room's amazing Sunday brunch will perk you right up.

Club Café – something the owners have embraced wholeheartedly, offering weekly drag events, including Glam Brunch bingo and *Drag Race* viewing parties.

DORCHESTER BREWING CO.

Map 5; 1250 Massachusetts Avenue, Dorchester; ///stages.lied.front; www.dorchesterbrewing.com

This gay-owned brewery is massive, queer-friendly, and brimming with fresh and flavorful craft brews. LGBTQ+ events are a hot commodity here, including Pride month kickoff parties and tea dances run by LesbianNightLife. But even if the calendar's empty, the open-air balcony and tasty IPAs make this place tough to pass up.

» Don't leave without snagging some decadent comfort food from on-site restaurant M&M BBQ (we love the honey hot chicken sando).

THE ALLEY BAR

Map 1; 14 Pl Alley, Downtown; ///nearly.unfair.congratulations; www.thealleybar.com

Not quite a dirty dive, yet far from polished, this two-story watering hole hasn't changed much since its debut in 2003. It continues to churn out cheap drinks to a loyal crowd of older bears, as well as host regular queer-focused events, which range from dazzling disco nights to gaymer get-togethers. Swing by to shoot some pool at one of the downstairs tables, get your groove on at the second-story dance floor, or sing your heart out at the weekly Sunday karaoke.

THE KARTAL

Map 2; 520 Tremont Street, South End; ///agent.deeper.sector;
www.thekartalboston.com

Filling the space left by the closure of the Boston Eagle, one of the city's most beloved gay bars, The Kartal has a lot to live up to. And while its classic cocktails and refined setting are a far cry from the grimy floors and cheap beer of the oh-so-grungy Eagle, this new bar is nevertheless winning over queer locals with its super-welcoming vibe.

JACQUES' CABARET

Map 2; 79 Broadway Street, Theater District; ///jars.booth.hello;
www.jacques-cabaret.com

Inspired by the rise of RuPaul, it feels as if every bar and restaurant in Boston is hosting a drag brunch or bingo. Yet this downtown gem has been doing it since your parents were in diapers. Opened in

No-frills Midway Cafe *(www. midwaycafe.com)* offers up entertainment every night of the week, bringing in Jamaica Plain locals with its stand-up comedy sessions and live music. Come Thursday, though, this storied JP dive bar plays host to Queeraoke. One of the city's longest-running queer nights, this event draws in talented vocalists and tone-deaf revelers alike, who come to belt out tune after tune with their friends.

1938, the pint-size venue began dabbling in drag in the 1970s and could definitely teach these up-and-comers a thing or two. Drag karaoke, open-mic comedy, and Broadway performances are just a few of the events that pop off on the twinkling, Christmas light-covered stage.

BLEND

Map 5; 1310 Dorchester Avenue, Dorchester; ///spoken.card.care; www.blenddorchester.com

This North Dorchester joint is morphing into one of the city's top queer hangouts. On any given day, you can find folk sipping local craft ales and noshing on fried pickles and veggie burgers. But the vibe isn't always so laid back. Come the weekend, DJs blast disco and pop into the wee hours.

CATHEDRAL STATION

Map 2; 1222 Washington Street, South End; ///hits.flats.nation; www.cathedralstation.com

Boston has some stellar LGBTQ+ spots for crushing vodka sodas to the sounds of Lady Gaga. But if you've got two left feet and a serious thirst for Pabst Blue Ribbon, Cathedral Station is your dream come true. Kick back with a game of darts or pool at this queer-friendly sports bar, or lounge on the sprawling outdoor patio with a drink.

» **Don't leave without** grabbing some of the bar's Bavarian Pretzel Twists to share. These salty treats come with either cheese sauce or Brown ale mustard for dipping.

Music Bars and Restaurants

It's not just concert venues that host live music in Boston. In fact, many of the city's bars and restaurants serve up live performances from local and national acts alongside drinks or dinner.

O'BRIEN'S PUB

Map 6; 3 Harvard Avenue, Allston; ///once.hood.hears; www.obrienspubboston.com

One of Boston's last strongholds for punk music, this bare-bones Irish pub hosts ear-shattering shows every night. Sure, the beer selection is pretty basic and the pub is as dark as a medieval dungeon – but that all adds to the charm, right?

MAD MONKFISH

Map 4; 524 Massachusetts Avenue, Cambridge; ///cats.glass.rich; www.themadmonkfish.com

Jazz and sushi might not be the most conventional couple, but Mad Monkfish makes it work a treat. Come the weekend, this Pan-Asian restaurant hosts intimate live jazz shows from a pint-size stage in its dining room. As sultry sounds strum through the air, an eclectic crowd snack on delicious caterpillar rolls and sushi, pausing occasionally to nod their heads to the music.

TOAD
Map 4; 1912 Massachusetts Avenue, Cambridge; ///loses.ideal.taped; www.toadcambridge.com

Once you've caught sight of that neon "TOAD" sign glowing in the window, you know you're in for a night of great music. Over the years, the bar's free, raucous rock shows have made it a favorite spot for longtime Cambridge hipsters. Music may be the main attraction, but don't sleep on the diverse craft beer list – an added bonus that keeps punters coming back on the reg.

LORETTA'S LAST CALL
Map 3; 1 Lansdowne Street, Fenway; ///signal.shiny.deal; www.lorettaslastcall.com

Pull on your cowboy boots and hotfoot it to Loretta's for a night of country music. Decorated with wagon-wheel chandeliers and pics of greats like Johnny Cash, this restaurant is all about toe-tapping country tunes – served with a side of hearty, Southern-style grub, of course. Inside, a mix of homesick Deep South transplants and country-loving loyalists munch on king-size plates of chicken and waffles, all while listening to a great lineup of country crooners.

» **Don't leave without** signing up for a line-dancing lesson, held on Tuesday and Sunday nights.

Solo, Pair, Crowd

Boston is bursting with Irish pubs that offer live music (and good craic) to longtime regulars and newbies alike.

FLYING SOLO
Settle in for a seisiún
The Burren, a snug Irish bar, is the perfect place for a chilled-out date with yourself. During the day, drop by to listen to laid-back Irish seisiúns, all while nursing a glass of Guinness.

IN A PAIR
Tunes for two
Cozy JP venue Brendan Behan has live Irish music performances each Saturday from 5pm to 8pm. It's the perfect spot for you and your other half to bond over the soothing sounds of the Emerald Isle.

FOR A CROWD
Bop to the beat
Thirsty Scholar Pub is a favorite of the Somerville crowd, who head here on Saturdays to head bop to live beats from local bands. Don't miss Reggae Night either, held every other Tuesday.

DARRYL'S CORNER BAR & KITCHEN

Map 3; 604 Columbus Avenue, Roxbury; ///empire.churn.pumps;
www.dcbkboston.com

Run by Nia Grace – cofounder of the Boston Black Hospitality
Coalition – Darryl's stands as a testament to Roxbury's rich Black
American heritage. Stellar live performances of soul, R&B, and jazz
are the norm at this legendary joint – as are dishes of delicious
savory soul food, including fried catfish and creole gumbo.

THE BEEHIVE

Map 2; 541 Tremont Street, South End; ///reveal.belong.trip;
www.beehiveboston.com

This South End hangout feels like a cross between a fancy bistro and a
lavish boudoir, thanks to its white tablecloths and red velvet curtains.
Step inside to rub shoulders with a ritzy crowd, who come to dine on
New American fare while listening to soulful jazz and lively funk music.
» Don't leave without snagging a resy for next weekend's jazz brunch,
where baked French toast and sultry tunes are the order of the day.

THE BEBOP

Map 3; 1116 Boylston Street, Back Bay; ///relate.sudden.truck;
www.beehiveboston.com

Located on the fringes of Back Bay, this little Irish pub is all about
easygoing jam sessions of bluegrass, jazz, and traditional Irish music.
Many events allow punters to participate, so bring along your sax
or fiddle and get ready to play some tunes.

Indie Theaters

Independent theater troupes and dance companies are big in Boston. There's plenty of entertainment, but many shows also challenge, inform, and initiate discussion – this is free-thinking Boston, after all.

SPEAKEASY STAGE COMPANY

Map 2; 539 Tremont Street, South End; ///sentences.plank.flag; www.speakeasystage.com

A big hit with South End and Back Bay theater buffs, this forward-thinking joint is all about thought-provoking works – the sort of plays and musicals that spark earnest conversations once the curtain closes. Taking place in an intimate space, past performances have covered topics as diverse as AIDS, autism, and race.

CENTRAL SQUARE THEATER

Map 4; 450 Massachusetts Avenue, Cambridge; ///gums.wonderfully.audit; www.centralsquaretheater.org

Two vanguard theaters for the price of one? Count us in. This joint is home to the Underground Railway Theater, which stages productions with an activist bent, and The Nora, focusing on contemporary pieces with a feminist perspective. Progressive Bostonians flock here to see engaging performances exploring everything from the power of female genius to the American Dream. Got your eye on an upcoming show? Don't wait to book – productions usually run for a month or less.

>> Don't leave without checking out the Youth Underground Festival, a multiday series of performances from aspiring high-school thespians.

LYRIC STAGE COMPANY

Map 2; 140 Clarendon Street, Back Bay; ///mason.dish.proof;
www.lyricstage.com

Back in the 1970s, curious locals visited a tiny second-floor space above a hardware store to see Lyric's production of *The Importance of Being Earnest*. It was so successful that bigger digs soon beckoned. Today, this theater company – the oldest in Boston – hosts award-winning takes on classics such as *My Fair Lady*, plus newer shows like *Fabulation* by Pulitzer-winning playwright Lynn Nottage.

Shh!

Time your visit to Boston right and you can indulge in some of the Bard's works alfresco, all courtesy of Shakespeare on the Common. Every year for two weeks in July, this local theater company stages a new Shakespearean play on an outdoor stage on the Boston Common – best of all, it's completely free to attend. Make like in-the-know locals and bring a picnic and blanket, then sit back and enjoy the show.

AMERICAN REPERTORY THEATER
Map 4; 64 Brattle Street, Harvard Square; ///couple.energy.begin;
www.americanrepertorytheater.org

This spot stages experimental plays and musicals, including some that have gone on to make it big on Broadway (we're looking at you, *Waitress*). It doesn't rest on its laurels, though, with a stream of new works addressing contemporary issues such as climate change.

» Don't leave without grabbing a post-performance cocktail at the super-sleek Longfellow Bar, just down the road from the theater.

URBANITY DANCE
Map 2; 725 Harrison Avenue, South End; ///sentences.incomes.lasted;
www.urbanitydance.org

Set up in 2011, Urbanity has brought contemporary dance to the forefront of Boston's art scene. The nonprofit puts on cutting-edge shows in venues across the city, with explosive original choreography that might incorporate anything from break dancing to modern jazz.

FRONT PORCH ARTS COLLECTIVE
Map 3; 527 Tremont Street, South End; ///sulk.tame.jump;
www.frontporcharts.org

Black writers, directors, and actors are the driving force behind Front Porch, Boston's first professional Black theater company. Shows here examine things like race, culture, and gender, with past performances including *Black Odyssey*, a retelling of Homer's epic tale with African American oral history and music.

Liked by the locals

"We wanted to contribute to Boston's wonderful theater scene by creating a home for Black voices and stories of the African Diaspora – one built on the work of the amazing Black theater companies and artists that came before us."

DAWN M. SIMMONS, CO-PRODUCING ARTISTIC DIRECTOR AT FRONT PORCH ARTS COLLECTIVE

An evening out in
Central Square

Laugh-out-loud comedy shows and long-standing music venues; Cambridge's Central Square is a lively hub for after-hours entertainment. Nestled between two world-famous universities, Harvard and MIT, the area's dynamic spirit is fueled by its bright-eyed students and creative faculty who work hard, play hard. Don't expect to be out too late, though – bars close at 2am on the dot here. Not that this stops revelers from letting loose before heading back to their dorms to finish up an essay.

1. A4cade
292 Massachusetts Avenue, Cambridge;
www.a4cade.com
///wacky.cook.crunch

2. Lamplighter Brewing
284 Broadway, Cambridge;
www.lamplighterbrewing.com
///suffer.pink.herds

3. ImprovBoston
620 Massachusetts Avenue, Cambridge;
www.improvboston.com
///potato.notice.wallet

4. Plough and Stars
912 Massachusetts Avenue, Cambridge; www.plough andstars.com
///digs.supper.opera

Graffiti Alley
///hang.worker.jobs

LEE STREET

4

Finish up at PLOUGH AND STARS
A short stroll northwest of Central Square, this welcoming Irish pub offers toe-tapping music and a lively atmosphere. What better way to round off your night?

WESTERN   AVENUE

STREET

RIVER

STREET

MAGAZINE

Dana Park

0 meters 200
0 yards 200

BROADWAY STREET

INMAN STREET

HARVARD STREET

PROSPECT STREET

Sennott Park

CAMBRIDGE

MASSACHUSETTS AVENUE

To get a sense of this neighborhood's creativity, check out Graffiti Alley, a public walkway covered in ever-changing street art.

NORFOLK STREET

BROADWAY

COLUMBIA STREET

WASHINGTON STREET

CENTRAL SQUARE

3

Laugh out loud at IMPROVBOSTON

Have a giggle at this Cambridge institution, which holds regular improv and stand-up sets from both big-name and local comics.

MAIN STREET

EARL STREET

BROOKLINE STREET

1

Start your night at A4CADE

Challenge your buddies to a classic 1980s video game (think Galaga), while chomping on a grilled cheese sandwich.

MASSACHUSETTS AVENUE

CAMBRIDGEPORT

2

Grab a drink at LAMPLIGHTER BREWING

Enjoy a creative craft brew or a hazy IPA at this cool spot; it's a favorite hangout for craft beer fans.

OUTDOORS

Whether taking a beachside amble, picnicking in the park, or paddling on the Charles River, Bostonians love being outside – even when the weather isn't playing ball.

Green Spaces

Arty esplanades, community-run gardens, pretty public parks – Boston is awash with green spaces. These urban oases are beloved by locals, who drop by to soak up a slice of nature.

BERKELEY COMMUNITY GARDEN

Map 2; enter at Tremont Street and Dwight Street, South End; ///option.tummy.grit; www.berkeleygardens.org

In the mid-1970s, some of South End's Chinese American community began guerilla gardening on an empty patch of ground. Fast-forward to today, the half-block plot is awash with life, and now a welcoming community hub where more than 140 gardeners grow beans, bitter melon, and more. Come by to watch these green-fingered folk at work; it's one of the few community gardens open to the public.

BOSTON PUBLIC GARDEN

Map 1; enter at Charles Street, Back Bay; ///stored.exist.rips; www.boston.gov/parks/public-garden

America's first botanical garden is a stunner. Here, you'll find wide, paved pathways winding past pretty flower beds, and a petite lagoon fringed by weeping willows and crossed by a stone-and-iron footbridge. Back Bay and Beacon Hill residents admire the scene on lunchtime strolls during the week, while on the weekends the garden is full of picnicking students and suburbanites.

» **Don't leave without** taking a ride on one of the iconic Swan Boats, which make trips around the park's pretty lagoon.

BOSTON COMMON

Map 1; enter at Tremont Street, Back Bay; ///inch.stays.stump; www.boston.gov/parks/boston-common

Founded in 1634, the oldest public park in the US has an inevitably rich history. It played host to colonial militia during the Revolution, anti-slavery meetings during the Civil War, and Civil Rights rallies in the 20th century. Oh, and did we mention it's the starting point for Boston's historic Freedom Trail *(p117)*? History aside, the park has plenty to recommend it: drop by in summer to play softball or tennis on one of the courts, or in winter to skate across the Frog Pond.

ARNOLD ARBORETUM

Map 6; 125 Arborway, Jamaica Plain; ///port.backed.prefer; www.arboretum.harvard.edu

North America's oldest public arboretum draws Bostonians year round, but spring is when it truly shines. As the weather warms, dusky pink roses, deep-orange azaleas, and lemon-yellow primroses burst into bloom here, there, and everywhere, putting on a kaleidoscopic show. The biggest spectacle happens in May, when more than 400 lilac plants blossom across the park in every hue of purple imaginable.

Solo, Pair, Crowd

In need of a solo sojourn? Planning an outdoor get-together with your best buds? Boston has a perfect park for everyone.

FLYING SOLO
Stroll for one

Whisk yourself away to the Urban Park Roof Garden, which sits on top of a parking garage in Cambridge's Kendall Square. Here you can take a chilled stroll among the miniature pine trees and raised flower beds.

IN A PAIR
Blossoming romance

The Kelleher Rose Garden is a dainty rose garden that blooms to full capacity during the warm, sunny days of June. Take your other half for a romantic walk under the blossom-covered trellises.

FOR A CROWD
Lawn party

Get your friends together for a trip to Lawn on D. Found in the middle of South Boston, this big patch of green has lots to entertain the gang, from lawn games to live music.

FRANKLIN PARK

Map 5; enter at Circuit Drive, Dorchester; ///page.living.drove;
www.boston.gov/parks/franklin-park

Boston's biggest park has everything you could ever want: paved woodland walking trails, a duck-dotted pond, and picnic-ready lawns. There's even an 18-hole golf course, where you'll find locals attempting hole-in-ones come rain, shine, or even a little snow.
» Don't leave without visiting the bear dens. Once part of Franklin Park Zoo, these long-abandoned cages have become a cult attraction.

ROSE KENNEDY GREENWAY

Map 1; enter at Sudbury Street and John F. Fitzgerald Surface Road,
Downtown; ///same.rear.dates; www.rosekennedygreenway.org

Replacing an old highway, this 7-mile- (11-km-) long park snakes around the edge of Boston's Downtown. Visit in summer, when you can wander past pretty flower beds and ever-changing art installations, before having a drink in the pop-up beer garden. Hungry? Grab a bite at one of the food trucks that often line the greenway.

PAUL REVERE PARK

Map 1; enter at North Washington Street, Charlestown;
///caves.camera.gift

Come summer, this patch of green at the mouth of the Charles River is buzzing. Families fly kites and couples enjoy sunny picnics, while dog owners watch as their pups race joyously across the flat, freshly mowed lawn. Bring a blanket and join in the fun.

By the Water

With the city cut through by three rivers and surrounded by ocean to the east, life in Boston is tied to the water. There are plenty of pretty waterside spots to discover, from golden beaches to riverside bike paths.

JOSEPH FINNEGAN PARK
Map 5; enter on Walnut Street, Dorchester; ///spaces.cubes.misty

For decades, this stretch along the Neponset River housed a dilapidated industrial complex. Then in the 1980s, a group of Dorchester locals, determined to revitalize the area, started a campaign to turn it into a waterfront park. A major restoration project kicked off and, 30 years later, this park is a local fave. Today, you'll find proud residents strolling past blossoming meadows and a wildlife-filled salt marsh.

DR. PAUL DUDLEY WHITE BIKE PATH
Map 1; start near the intersection of Edwin H. Land Boulevard and Cambridge Parkway, Cambridge; ///fear.loser.trout

Jump on your cycling steed and explore this looping path that traces both banks of the Charles River. There's lots to see on the water as you cruise, from elegant sail boats in summer to crew teams training for the Head of the Charles Regatta *(p178)* in fall. Tackle the full 17-mile

(27-km) route, if you fancy, or gently pedal the 4-mile (6-km) slice from the Museum of Science (p124) to Harvard Bridge and back. The city views are really dreamy.

The City of Boston has a cycling section on its website, complete with a bike map (www.boston.gov).

SYLVESTER BAXTER RIVERFRONT PARK

Map 6; enter at Great River Road, Somerville; ///nurses.brave.hike

Locals love heading to this waterside park for an easygoing amble. If you fancy joining them, start on the east side of the park by the playground (a hot spot for young families), then stroll west along the shaded paths. A highlight is the wooden boardwalk that curves over the water, offering views across the boat-dotted Mystic River to the tree-shrouded banks on the other side.

REVERE BEACH

Map 6; enter at Revere Beach Boulevard, Revere;
///unrealistic.chest.cheat; www.reverebeach.com

Set up in 1896, Revere is famed for being the first public beach in the US, but that's not why you'll want to visit. During the annual International Sand Sculpting Festival, in July, professional sand sculptors descend on this long sliver of beach to make weird and wonderful sculptures. Past creations have included a triceratops head, a historic ship, and, of course, a castle (complete with soaring turrets, no less). Better grab your bucket and start practicing.

» **Don't leave without** stopping in at nearby Kelly's (350 Revere Beach Boulevard) for one of its famous roast beef sandwiches.

BOSTON HARBOR ISLANDS NATIONAL AND STATE PARK

Map 6; ferry from Long Wharf, Downtown; ///casual.shell.sleepy; www.bostonharborislands.org

After some peace and quiet? Boston's Harbor Islands will do the trick. Sprinkled just off the city's east coast, these 34 protected isles are a world away from Boston's bustle. Head to Spectacle Island (p174) to lounge on golden sands, or hop over to Tompson Island to spy egrets and herons in the salt marshes. The trip there by public ferry is pretty cool, too, offering fab views of both the islands and Boston's cityscape.

KAYAK ON THE CHARLES RIVER

Map 4; Charles River Canoe & Kayak, 15 Broad Canal Way, Cambridge; ///sugars.dose.jacket; www.paddleboston.com

If you're after a new perspective on Boston, take a paddle on the Charles. Not only will you get a swan's-eye view of the city skyline, you'll also spy a floating wetland, a patch of plants created to improve the river's ecosystem. Rent a kayak from Charles River Canoe & Kayak, a short paddle from the wetland, and get exploring.

TENEAN BEACH

Map 5; enter off Conley Street, Dorchester; ///diner.organ.enjoy; www.mass.gov/locations/tenean-beach

Hugging the edge of the Neponset River, this patch of sand is a little pocket of paradise. Its golden shores are the perfect place for a lazy sunbathe, while the surrounding blue waters are great for a laid-back dip. But it's not all about the chill here. Fitness-focused locals also love the beach for its basketball and tennis courts, plus its easy access to the Neponset Trail that runs alongside the river.

» Don't leave without checking out Corita Kent's "Rainbow Swash," a series of rainbow streaks painted on a massive natural gas tank. It's the largest copyrighted work of art in the world.

CHARLES RIVER ESPLANADE

Map 3; enter via the Arthur Fiedler Footbridge, Back Bay;
///cages.order.cove; www.esplanade.org

Come the first warm day of spring, locals hotfoot it to this slender park hugging the edge of the Charles River. Why? Well, there's a whole laundry list of reasons, from enjoying an alfresco concert to sipping suds in Night Shift Brewing's *(p72)* pop-up beer garden. Really, though, there's no need to do anything other than sit shoulder-to-shoulder on the dock, watching as the sun sinks slowly over the river.

CARSON BEACH

Map 5; enter at William J. Day Boulevard, South Boston;
///moods.prop.dust; www.mass.gov/locations/castle-island-pleasure-
bay-m-street-beach-and-carson-beach

Perched on the western shore of Boston's Old Harbor, this beach is ultra-popular in summer. Spot a young crowd soaking up the rays, drinks in hand, while groups of yogis stretch out on the sand. It's busy, but there's plenty of room to spread out; Carson links up with neighboring beaches to form one huge sandy arc.

Wonderful Walks

Fun fact: the city of Boston has one of the highest step counts in the US (even with those bone-chilling winters). And with such picturesque parks and charming streets, we can easily see why.

OLMSTED PARK

Map 3; start at Jamaicaway, Mission Hill; ///frosted.crest.blaze; www.emeraldnecklace.org/park-overview/olmsted-park

As the weather grows warmer, Mission Hill locals emerge from their apartments to bask in the beauty of Olmsted Park. Join them on a wander along the park's pretty paths, which wind through groves of budding trees and past a series of tranquil, bird-filled ponds.

BOSTON HARBORWALK

Map 1; start at William J. Day Boulevard, South Boston; ///worker.badly.spoken; www.bostonharbornow.org/what-we-do/ explore/harborwalk

Fancy a weekend walking sesh? Then this route is for you. Stretching for 43 miles (69 km), this coastal promenade runs from the mouth of the Neponset River in Dorchester to sandy Constitution Beach in East Boston. While walking pros (and folks training for the marathon) might tackle the whole lot, more gentle amblers will be happy with a smaller section. Try the South Boston stretch, which winds past iconic sights like the John F. Kennedy Presidential Library and Museum *(p125)*.

# MIDDLESEX FELLS RESERVATION
Map 6; start at S Border Road, Stoneham; ///along.wallet.beams; www.mass.gov/locations/middlesex-fells-reservation

The Fells, as locals call it, is where folks go to get their blood pumping. This sprawling slice of green is loaded with picturesque lakes, dense oak forests, and a whole lot of craggy cliffs. While mountain bikers hit the trails and kayakers take to the water, hikers head for the Rock Circuit Trail. This 4.6-mile (7.5-km) forest loop can be a challenge, it's true, thanks to exposed tree roots and rocky sections. But the stunning views across the park will keep you going for miles.

» Don't leave without kicking back at Straw Point, a sandy stretch of beach overlooking Spot Pond, with a posthike picnic.

# ACORN STREET
Map 1; start at Willow Street, Beacon Hill; ///agreed.venue.tiger

Nestled within historic Beacon Hill, this narrow little street is the undisputed belle of Boston, thanks to its gleaming cobblestones, old-school gas lamps, and Federal-style houses. Sure, it's not the longest of walks; the street is only one twentieth of a mile. But it's still surprisingly easy to while away time here, stopping to admire the lane's good looks (it's earned the title of Boston's most photographed street, don't you know).

SPECTACLE ISLAND

Map 6; start at Spectacle Island Visitors Center, Spectacle Island;
///chain.losses.nearly; www.bostonharborislands.org

Don't be put off by the fact that Spectacle Island served as a giant
dump until the 1990s – this green isle in the Boston Harbor has really
cleaned up its act. Today, locals whizz over on the public ferry to roam
the island's trails, which cut through wildflower-laden meadows and
hilly pastures. Wherever you walk, beautiful ocean views are a given.

COMMONWEALTH AVENUE MALL

Map 3; start at Hereford Street, Back Bay; ///puns.define.begun;
www.boston.gov/parks/commonwealth-avenue-mall

Whatever the season, this French-style boulevard is a hit with locals,
who come to stroll the tree-lined paths. In spring, the mall's freshly
budding trees draw in walkers, while come fall, it's the beauty of the

Shh!

Okay, Harvard Bridge is pretty
famous, but not many people
know that it's the birthplace of
"smoots." This bizarre unit of
measurement dates back to
1958, when MIT student Oliver
Smoot lay down at intervals
across the entire bridge while
his peers used him as a make-
shift ruler. Take a stroll across
this lengthy bridge and you'll
have walked 364.4 smoots –
that's just over 2,030 ft (620 m)
to the rest of us.

Bay State's crimson foliage that lures them in. And in winter? Well, who can resist the magical sight of snow-covered branches strung with golden fairy lights?

BOSTON NATURE CENTER

Map 5; 500 Walk Hill Street, Mattapan; ///calms.super.lists; www.massaudubon.org/boston

Nestled in the heart of Mattapan, this verdant urban park (run by Mass Audubon, a nonprofit nature charity) is a wildlife hot spot. Bostonians pop in for weekend walks, binoculars in hand, in the hope of glimpsing songbirds flitting across lush meadows or turtles hiding in the tangled wetlands.

PLEASURE BAY

Map 6; start at William J. Day Boulevard, South Boston; ///third.budget.yard; www.mass.gov/locations/castle-island-pleasure-bay-m-street-beach-and-carson-beach

This Southie beach is where it's at come summer: yogis stretch out on the sand, families chat over picnics, and windsurfers speed across the water. Take in the scene with an amble around the Pleasure Bay Loop. This 2-mile (3-km) trail heads along the beach before winding across the causeway that encircles the bay. Once you've hit Head Island, take a beat to enjoy the great views back toward the city.

>> Don't leave without taking a tour of Fort Independence on Castle Island, found at the far end of the causeway. This massive star-shaped military outpost was established in 1634.

Live Sports Venues

Baseball, football, ice hockey, basketball – all sport is sacred in Boston. Come game day, dedicated fans head to the city's premier stadiums to cheer on their teams (and pray for a victory).

CRIMSON AT HARVARD STADIUM

Map 4; 79 N Harvard Street, Allston; ///pretty.bank.apple; www.gocrimson.com

Gamedays at this iconic college stadium are always electric. As the boys in red take to the field, marching bands strike up tunes, and students and alumni cheer wildly. The atmosphere is at its most charged during the much-anticipated game against the Yale Bulldogs, their arch rivals, when students from both sides get

Try it!
ENJOY A GAME

LoPresti Park in East Boston is the perfect spot to play a casual game of soccer or basketball with a group of friends – all while taking in stunning views over the city center.

creative with cheeky banners and signs. You don't need to be a student to watch, so pull on a crimson sweater and get ready to belt out "Ten Thousand Men of Harvard" with the best of them.

BRUINS AND CELTICS AT TD GARDEN

Map 1; 100 Legends Way, West End; ///jaws.patrol.book;
www.tdgarden.com

Whether it's the Celtics shooting hoops or the Bruins speeding across the ice, this vast arena is always packed with roaring fans. And they have a lot to shout about: both teams have won multiple championships in the past and are currently the top dogs in their respective leagues. Come by for a game (the court switches between wood and ice depending on who's playing), jumping up and down wildly alongside the die-hard supporters whenever a point is scored.

PATRIOTS AT GILLETTE STADIUM

Map 6; 1 Patriot Place, Foxborough; ///spurted.recruitment.slider;
www.gilettestadium.com

Despite not technically being in Boston proper (in fact, it's about half an hour away in Foxborough), this stadium still makes the cut. Why? It's the home of Boston's beloved New England Patriots, of course. On even the coldest winter days, staunch supporters crowd in – wearing Pats jerseys over their thick sweatshirts and parkas – all hoping for another Super Bowl win.

>> Don't leave without planning to join die-hard soccer fans at a New England Revolution game; this team also calls Gillette Stadium home.

HEAD OF THE CHARLES REGATTA

Map 3; 619 Memorial Drive, Cambridge; ///wasp.oils.dragon; www.hocr.org

In fall, locals flock to the banks and footbridges of the Charles River. Why? For this famous regatta, of course. Here, fleets of crew teams race as fast as they can down the river toward the finish line at Herter Park, whipped up by the cheers of the crowd.

RED SOX AT FENWAY PARK

Map 3; 4 Yawkey Way, Fenway; ///kind.trash.drag;
www.mlb.com/redsox/ballpark

There's oodles of nostalgia at Fenway. The oldest Major League ballpark in the US has countless nods to its 100-year-plus past, including a hand-turned scoreboard. As for the fans, passionate doesn't begin to cover it. Come game day, generations of Bostonians descend on the bleachers to root for the Red Sox (and grumble about the Yankees), singing "Sweet Caroline" at the tops of their voices.

» Don't leave without seeing the famous "red seat," which marks where the longest home run in the stadium's history landed.

BOSTON PRIDE AT WARRIOR ICE ARENA

Map 6; 90 Guest Street, Brighton; ///mild.stops.takes;
www.warricearena.com

The Bruins might practice here, but the real stars are the Boston Pride, the city's championship-winning women's hockey team. Their supporters are a welcoming bunch, who will strike up a convo with anyone, even fans of the rival team – you're all women's hockey fans, after all.

Liked by the locals

"During tours, I often refer to
Fenway as a museum where
baseball just happens to be played.
When looking at the field, you can
almost feel the presence of past
Red Sox teams, good and bad, and
of all of the great players that
have graced the stadium."

MATTHEW GINNETTY, TOUR GUIDE AT FENWAY PARK

Nearby Getaways

Bostonians are proud of their city, but even they need a change of scenery once in a while. Luckily, the historic towns, scenic shores, and forested mountains of New England are all right on their doorstep.

White Mountains
90 miles (145 km)

NEW HAMPSHIRE

Nashua

Newburyport

Ipswich

Rockport

Lowell

Gloucester

Gardner

Atlantic Ocean

Leominster

Salem

Concord

Lynn

MASSACHUSETTS

BOSTON

Stellwagen Bank National Marine Sanctuary

Worcester

Framingham

Quincy

Blue Hills Reservation

Scituate

Sturbridge

Provincetown

Attleboro

Plymouth

CONNECTICUT

RHODE ISLAND

Cape Cod Bay

Taunton

0 kilometers 40

Providence

Sandwich

Cape Cod

0 miles 40

ROCKPORT

1.5-hour train ride from the city; www.rockportusa.com

In the 19th century, this little seaside town was a buzzing artists' enclave; today, it's crammed with galleries showcasing local works. Budding creators day-trip here when they need some inspo or want to chat with like-minded artists (many of whom run their own galleries).

SALEM

30-minute train ride from the city; www.salem.org

There's more to Salem than its spooktacular Halloween celebrations. This town is chock-full of sights dedicated to its rich – and sometimes harrowing – history. Drop by the Salem Maritime National Historic Site to uncover its seafaring past or visit the Salem Witch Museum to learn about the infamous trials that took place here in 1692. After, mull everything over with a walk along the town's cobbled streets.

CAPE COD

1.5-hour ferry from the city to Provincetown; www.capecodchamber.org

White-sand beaches, pretty seaside villages, and super-fresh seafood: no wonder this sweeping peninsula is such a popular summer hang-out. Getting here is easy for Bostonians, too; just a short ferry ride from the city, on the tip of the cape, is Provincetown, a small community known for its thriving LGBTQ+ culture. Weekend escape, anyone?

» Don't leave without visiting the Provincetown Museum's exhibit on the early history of the Wampanoag. Told in the group's own words, it covers their complicated relationship with the Mayflower Pilgrims.

BLUE HILLS RESERVATION

30-minute drive from the city

When locals get tired of city life, they hotfoot it to this scenic reserve for some outdoor adventure. Here, mountain bikers zoom through forest, climbers scale near-vertical walls, and hikers head for rocky summits. Once they're done, it's off to Houghton's Pond for a refreshing dip.

IPSWICH

1-hour train ride from the city

Want a bite of heaven? You'll find it in Ipswich. This waterside town is famous for its fried clams, which come encased in golden batter. Woodman's is the place to try them; this mouthwatering dish was invented by the restaurant's original owner, Lawrence "Chubby" Woodman, around a century ago. Grab a load of these crispy bites and eat them while strolling along pretty Crane Beach.

WHITE MOUNTAINS

2.5-hour drive from the city; www.visitwhitemountains.com

Covered with deep-green forest and dotted by roaring waterfalls, this range of rugged peaks makes the perfect getaway for work-weary locals. Countless trails lace through the area, ideal for hiking, mountain biking, and horseback riding, while tranquil lakes offer the

Shh!

Found a stone's throw west of the quaint town of Newburyport, Maudslay State Park is a quiet haven beloved by locals. Folk flock here to stroll through the 19th-century gardens or picnic on the rolling meadows. There are lots of opportunities to bird-watch among the pines, too; the park is home to a whole bunch of feathered friends, among them great horned owls and bald eagles. Just remember to pack those binoculars.

chance to canoe and kayak. If the thought of that tires you out, hop on the area's historic cog railroad for an easy ride up Mount Washington, which offers some truly eye-popping views of the surrounding hills.

PLYMOUTH

1-hour bus ride from the city; www.seeplymouth.com

In 1620, the first Puritan settlers arrived here from England on the *Mayflower*, establishing a settlement that would eventually become the oldest in the state. Today, visitors from far and wide descend on this historic coastal city, the birthplace of Massachusetts, to wander its historic streets and explore the *Mayflower II*, a replica of the famous wooden ship.

» Don't leave without visiting Historic Patuxet, where descendants of the area's original inhabitants, the Wampanoag, chat about their history and culture, and showcase traditional activities like canoe building.

STELLWAGEN BANK NATIONAL MARINE SANCTUARY

4-hour round trip from Long Wharf, Downtown; www.neaq.org/exhibits/whale-watch

Those wanting to see spouting humpbacks and breaching minke whales have come to the right place. From May to October, this protected stretch of saltwater off Boston's coast is sprinkled with migrating cetaceans. Take a tour organized by the New England Aquarium, where expert naturalists are on hand to provide insight into the behavior and anatomy of different species.

Pause at the
FROG POND

During the hot summers, local families descend on the spray pool to cool off. In the winter, it's time to ice-skate across the pond's frozen surface.

The **Ether Monument** *marks a slightly obscure part of history: the use of ether (in its gas form) as a general anesthetic.*

Snap a photo of
MAKE WAY FOR DUCKLINGS

These super-cute sculptures are based on a kids' book about a family of ducks searching for a new home.

Boston Public Garden

Boston Common

Take a ride on the
SWAN BOATS

Enjoy a trip around the Public Garden's weeping willow-lined lagoon on one of these iconic swan-shaped boats.

Grab breakfast at
TATTE BAKERY & CAFÉ

Enjoy a hearty breakfast at this beloved brunch spot (the meze's a winner). Pick up a sandwich, too – you'll want it later for a picnic on the Common.

BEACON HILL

CHARLES STREET

BEACON STREET

CHARLES STREET

ARLINGTON STREET

BOYLSTON STREET

PARK PLAZA

BOYLSTON STREET

CHARLES STREET

STREET

TREMONT STREET

STUART STREET

SOUTH

0 meters 200
0 yards 200

Granary
Burying
Ground

The 17th-century
Granary Burying
Ground *is the resting*
place of famous citizens
such as Samuel Adams
and Paul Revere.

Make for the start of
THE FREEDOM TRAIL
spend the rest of the day
tackling this historical 2.5-mile
(4-km) walking route; it starts
right here on the eastern edge
of Boston Common.

ESSEX STREET

STUART STREET

CHINATOWN

A morning stroll through
Boston Common and Public Garden

These adjoining urban oases are two of the biggest jewels in Boston's Emerald Necklace, an extensive chain of parks that loop from the city's east side to its west. That's not their only claim to fame – they were also the first public park and first botanical garden (respectively) in the US. Pop by any day and you'll find locals taking a lunchtime walk, playing a game of baseball or tennis, or picnicking on the grass with a book in hand.

1. Tatte Bakery & Café
70 Charles Street, Beacon
Hill; www.tattebakery.com
///enter.basin.hunter

2. Swan Boats
Boston Public Garden, Back
Bay; www.swanboats.com
///gown.accent.enter

3. Make Way for Ducklings
Boston Public Garden, Back
Bay; www.schon.com/public/
ducklings-boston.php
///patch.hands.nuns

4. Frog Pond
Boston Common,
Beacon Hill; www.
bostonfrogpond.com
///leaves.fails.chief

5. The Freedom Trail
Boston Common, Beacon
Hill; www.thefreedomtrail.org
///plots.given.desire

Granary Burying Ground
///ants.enjoyable.melt

Ether Monument
///agreed.penny.school

With a little research and preparation, this city will feel like a home away from home. Check out these websites to ensure a healthy, safe stay in Boston.

Boston
DIRECTORY

SAFE SPACES

Boston is a diverse and welcoming city, but should you feel uneasy at any point or want to find your community, there are plenty of spaces and resources to help you out.

www.bagly.org
BAGLY is a social-support organization that offers assistance to LGBTQ+ youth.

www.blackownedbos.com
A curated directory of Black-owned businesses operating in the city.

www.bostonjcc.org
A Jewish cultural community center providing cultural and social programs.

www.mccboston.org
An inclusive queer-centric church serving Boston's LGBTQ+ community.

HEALTH

Health care in the US isn't free, so it's important to take out comprehensive health insurance for your visit. If you do need medical assistance, Boston is known for its world-class medical care.

www.cvs.com
A pharmacy chain with locations across Boston; many are open 24 hours.

www.fenwayhealth.org
Fenway Health offers health-care services for Boston's LGBTQ+ community.

www.massgeneralbrigham.org
The largest and best-known hospital network in Massachusetts.

www.namimass.org
A nonprofit organization supporting those affected by mental illness.

www.massmed.org
A comprehensive list of free medical clinics throughout Massachusetts.

www.plannedparenthood.org/health-center/massachusetts
Nonprofit organization providing sexual health care for all.

TRAVEL SAFETY INFORMATION
Before you travel – and while you're here – always keep tabs on the latest regulations in Boston, and the US.

www.bpdnews.com
The official website of the Boston police department. It provides information on how to report crimes in the area.

www.bpl.org/emergency-help-and-hotlines
List of emergency help and hotline numbers serving the city and state.

www.cdc.gov
Public health organization offering advice on disease prevention.

www.cityofboston.gov/students/safety
City government-curated list of safety resources for locals and travelers.

www.Mass511.com
A free statewide traveler information service that provides live traffic reports.

ACCESSIBILITY
Boston has made great strides in accessibility, but with lots of historic sights and cobbled streets, it's not always the easiest to navigate. These resources will help make your visit go more smoothly.

www.deafinconline.com
Resources for the deaf and hearing-impaired community in Boston.

www.mbta.com/accessibility
List of accessible MBTA stations (with live elevator and escalator status), and other accessible travel information.

www.mass.gov/orgs/massachusetts-commission-for-the-blind
Resources for Boston's blind and visually impaired communities.

www.mass.gov/service-details/accessibility-resources
A list of general accessibility resources recommended by the local government.

www.tdgarden.com/accessibility
An accessibility guide to the TD Garden, one of Boston's busiest venues.

INDEX

ACKNOWLEDGMENTS

Meet the illustrator

*Award-winning British illustrator
David Doran is based in a studio by the sea
in Falmouth, Cornwall. When not drawing
and designing, David tries to make the
most of the beautiful area in which he's
based; sea-swimming all year round,
running the coastal paths, and generally
spending as much time outside as possible.*

Main Contributors Meaghan Agnew,
Cathryn Haight, Jared Ranahan

Senior Editor Lucy Richards

Senior Designer Stuti Tiwari Bhatia

Project Editor Rachel Laidler

Project Art Editor Bharti Karakoti

US Editor Jennette ElNaggar

Editors Alex Pathe, Danielle Watt

Designer Jordan Lambley

Proofreader Kathryn Glendenning

Indexer Helen Peters

Senior Cartographic Editor Casper Morris

Cartography Manager Suresh Kumar

Cartographer Ashif

Jacket Designers Jordan Lambley, Sarah Snelling

Jacket Illustrator David Doran

Senior Production Editor Jason Little

Senior Production Controller Samantha Cross

Managing Editor Hollie Teague

Managing Art Editor Sarah Snelling

Art Director Maxine Pedliham

Publishing Director Georgina Dee

MIX
Paper | Supporting
responsible forestry
FSC™ C018179

This book was made with
Forest Stewardship Council™
certified paper – one small step
in DK's commitment to a
sustainable future.
**For more information go to
www.dk.com/our-green-pledge**

A NOTE FROM DK EYEWITNESS

The world is fast-changing and it's keeping us folk at
DK Eyewitness on our toes. We've worked hard to ensure
that this edition of Boston Like a Local is up-to-date and
reflects today's favourite places but we know that standards
shift, venues close and new ones pop up in their place. So, if
you notice something has closed, we've got something
wrong or left something out, we want to hear about it.
Please drop us a line at travelguides@dk.com

First edition 2023

Published in Great Britain by Dorling Kindersley Limited,
DK, One Embassy Gardens, 8 Viaduct Gardens,
London SW11 7BW, UK

The authorised representative in the EEA is
Dorling Kindersley Verlag GmbH. Arnulfstr.
124, 80636 Munich, Germany

Published in the United States by DK Publishing,
1745 Broadway, 20th Floor, New York, NY 10019, USA

Copyright © 2023 Dorling Kindersley Limited
A Penguin Random House Company
23 24 25 26 10 9 8 7 6 5 4 3 2 1

A CIP catalog record for this book is available from the British Library.
A catalog record for this book is available from the Library of Congress.
ISSN: 1542 1554
ISBN: 9780 2416 3307 6
Printed and bound in China.
www.dk.com